An Illustrated History of

M & G N J R

Locomotives

Frontispiece: **The Spirit of Melton Works – Johnson 4-4-0 No. 5, built by Sharp, Stewart for the Midland & Great Northern Joint Railway in 1894.**

From coupler-flange to spindle-guide I see thy hand, O God -
Predestination in the stride o' yon connectin' rod.
The crank-throws give the double-bass, the feed-pump sobs an' heaves
An' now the main eccentrics start their quarrel on the sheaves:

Rudyard Kipling

An Illustrated History of

M & G N J R
Locomotives

by

Ronald H. Clark
M.I.Mech.E.

Past President, The Newcomen Society.
President & Chairman, The M.&G.N. Circle

Oxford Publishing Co.

To The
Immortal Memory
of
George Stephenson
1781-1848

A FOULIS-OPC Railway Book

British Library Cataloguing in Publication Data
Clark, Ronald H. (Ronald Harry), *1903—*
Illustrated history of Midland & Great Northern
Locomotives.
1. Great Britain. Steam Locomotives, history
I. Title
625.2610941
ISBN 0-86093-434-9

Library of Congress catalog card number
90-82080

Published by:
Haynes Publishing Group
Sparkford, Near Yeovil, Somerset. BA22 7JJ

Haynes Publications Inc.
861 Lawrence Drive, Newbury Park, California 91320, USA.

Printed by: J.H. Haynes & Co. Ltd

Contents

List of Drawings

The Prefatorial Remarks

I REMEMBER the M & GN when a small boy, just before World War One. I adored all their locomotives, resplendent in their Golden Gorse. In later years I used the system frequently, and when working in Lynn Regis, travelled on both the "Leicester" and local stopping trains. The saddest occasion was Lynn and back from Norwich City on the last "Leicester", 28th February 1959. It was hard to accept that no longer could I, or you, book to Bluestone, South Lynn or Twenty. Admittedly, the Joint could not take me elsewhere in East Anglia, but one of George Brough's luxurious vee twins provided my obvious alternative transport.

The locomotive aspect was always alluring and accounted for many official, and unofficial, visits to Melton Works, From my drawing office window in the works at South Lynn I could often watch No.93 when traversing one particular siding. Another friend was No.97 in Norwich City goods yard. My harem consisted of all the "Peacocks" – what a delightful outline and broadside prospect the final forms provided. If many women have some charm, some source of unexplained delight, the Peacocks certainly had their share. I respected too the Johnsonian outlines of both goods and passenger and I felt the same for the more rugged looking Ivatt contribution.

Having been responsible for two books on the Joint as a railway, it dawned on me its mixed and historic locomotive engines deserved a book to themselves. Hence this volume. If such a book is to be kept within reasonable bounds – proportionate to its selling price – then one cannot include every small detail of every type. But I hope the builder's drawings, personally redrawn and coloured according to the contemporary colour code for materials and made suitable for reproduction, will provide many details not mentioned in my text, or elsewhere. Regarding the other illustrations the problem was deciding what to include and what to omit. Several photographs and drawings have been included with the model maker in mind.

As many readers will know, the Eastern & Midlands Railway (E&MR) was created by the amalgamation of three or more small local Norfolk lines and each company had bought engines of various types and from different builders. The result was a rather motley but nonetheless attractive and interesting collection of prime movers. The 32 at work at the time of the formation of the E&MR in 1883 would merit a book of their own, irrespective of those acquired by the Joint after its formation in 1893. The system started off with an engineer of great charm, character and professional prowess in charge and to whom proper maintenance was paramount. This accounts in no small measure for the feats of haulage accomplished by comparatively lightweight engines and the absence of mechanical clatter when so doing. Such work was carried on very ably by his successors.

I am not so sanguine as to think that in my text there are no errors – it's amazing how they will creep in – so I hope if any are found my friends will report them so that in the event of another edition they can be corrected. I must remind the reader that many minor alterations and modifications were performed at Melton, many without being officially recorded. It is likely therefore that it could be pointed out that there are some small omissions covering minor mechanical features I have not listed, so I felt it advisable to mention this aspect of Melton's maintenance and re-building.

Information has been gleaned from a variety of sources and my thanks are due to many members of the M. & G.N. Circle and to this organisation as a whole for allowing me to use some material from the Circle's Bulletins and from their photographic collection. Many illustrations are from my own and my late father's (H.O. Clark) collections. I must thank the late Percy Youngman and Mrs P. Youngman for *Plate 55*, R.Meek Esq. for *Plate 20*, J.Plummer Esq. for *Plate 44*, and R.Whitehead Esq. for *Plate 17*. Should I by chance have infringed unknowingly anyone's copyright or similar, then it was quite unintentional and because of no written information concerning its origin.

Then there are the several manufacturers I have visited and who have helped me with information and technical data over the years including Messrs Beyer, Peacock & Co. Ltd, the late John Alcock of the Hunslet Engine Co., the late Wilfred Peckett, the North British Locomotive Co., the late Lt. Col. E. Kitson Clark and several others. All were most helpful. Also, thanks to *The Engineer* for the reproduction of the engraving of CMR No.14.

I am most grateful also to the following private persons who have allowed me to make use of their extensive knowledge, viz Mrs P Youngman, Raymond Meek Esq., A. Macfarlane Wells Esq., G. Yeomans Esq., the late Arthur Attoe Esq., Michael R. Lane Esq., the late Paul C. Dewhurst Esq., and several others. To all the above I am indebted and to those also mentioned in the text.

The M & GN (save for a few hundred chains in North Norfolk) has gone forever and lately one of the three 'A' framed bridges nigh unto Norwich was wantonly destroyed by an authority which should have known better. I hope therefore this volume will help the younger readers who never knew the "Joint" to appreciate how efficiently it was run and what a "matey" kind of delightful railway it really was.

Ronald H. Clark
Shotesham All Saints
Norwich.

I

The Bristol Rovers

VERY QUICKLY after the passing of the Act of June 1876 sanctioning the Great Yarmouth & Stalham Light Railway (GY&SLR), an order was placed that month with Messrs Fox, Walker & Co., of the Atlas Engine Works, Saint George, Bristol. At this period the firm had gained no little publicity through making a number of successful steam tram engines for home and abroad and the directors of the Yarmouth line were obviously sufficiently impressed to ask Messrs Fox, Walker to tender. This tender was successful and the two 0-6-0 saddle tank locomotives, builder's numbers 333 and 338 and named *Ormesby* and *Stalham* respectively, eventually came to Norfolk. It is here appropriate to note that Messrs Fox, Walker made a total of 410 locomotive engines before they were taken over by Thomas Peckett in 1880, the combination now bearing the title Peckett & Sons, Atlas Engine Works, Bristol.

The drawings from which I have prepared *Fig.1* are dated 15th August 1877 (on drawing No.1757 the draughtsman's initials being W.A) and the builders designated these engines as their Type B1. The main dimensions of these two B1s are as follows:

Cylinders	13in x 20in
Driving wheels, dia.	3ft 7in
Wheelbase – leading to driving	4ft 10in
Wheelbase – driving to trailing	4ft 10in
Wheelbase – total	9ft 8in
Working pressure.	140 psi
Rail to underside of footplate	3ft 9in
Rail to CL of boiler	5ft 3in
Rail to CL of buffers	3ft 3in
Rail to top of chimney	10ft 9in
Length over buffers	22ft 6in
Tank capacity	550gall
Fuel capacity	25cwt
Weight in W.O.	24ton 10cwt
Tractive effort @ 80%	8,907lb

It is illuminating here to record from contemporary reports, how these engines were delivered to the new railway, having no physical connection with the GER. They were sent on rail with coupling rods removed and in due course *Ormesby* was the first to arrive, the GER delivering it to the Hall Quay on 9th May

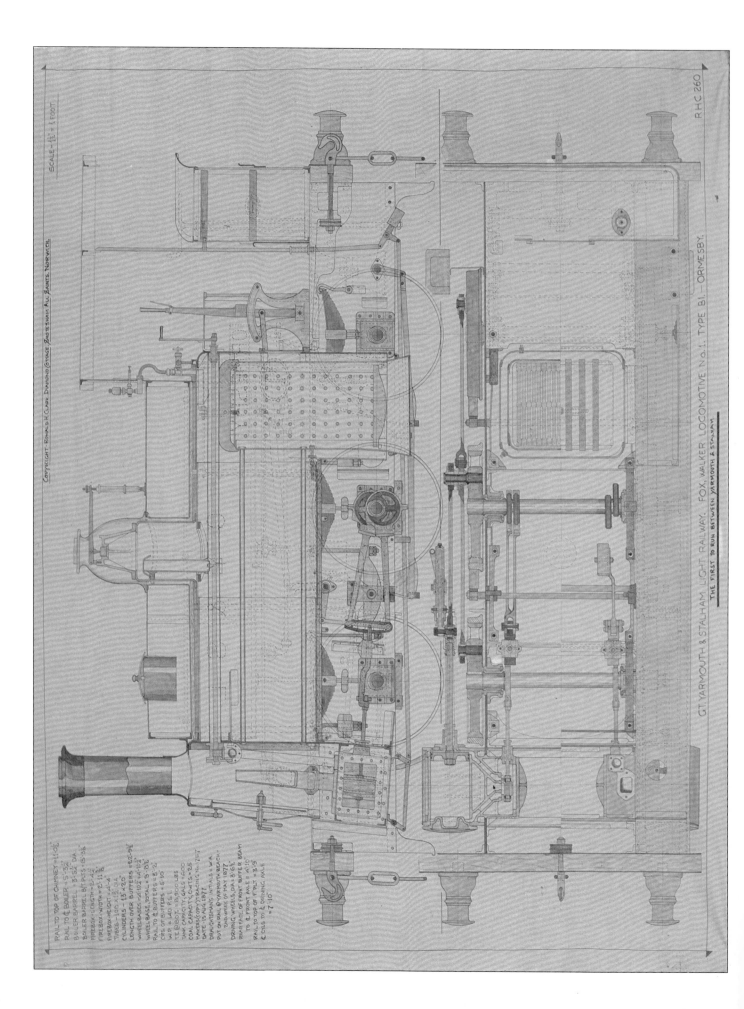

SCALE — $1\frac{1}{2}'' = 1$ FOOT.

R.H.C. 260

RAIL TO TOP OF CHIMNEY = 11'-0½"
RAIL TO ₵ BOILER = 5'-3½"
BOILER BARREL = 3'-5½" DIA.
BOILER BARREL B/T PLTS = 8'-3¾"
FIREBOX LENGTH = 2'-4½"
FIREBOX WIDTH = 2'-11⅛"
FIREBOX HEIGHT = 4'-4"
TUBES = 100 × 1¾" DIA.
CYLINDERS = 13" × 20"
LENGTH OVER BUFFERS = 22'-9½"
WHEELBASES = 6'-10½" + 4'-10½"
WHEEL BASE, TOTAL = 9'-9½"
RAIL TO ₵ BUFFERS = 3'-2"
CRS. OF BUFFERS = 5'-10"
W.P. = 140 P.S.I.
W.T. @ BOX. = 13,300 LBS
TANK CAPACITY, GALS = 600
COAL CAPACITY, CWTS = 25
WKS. No. COPY/TRACING No. 1707
DATE 15 AUG 1877.
DRAUGHTSMANS INITIALS = W.A.
PUT ON RAIL @ YARMOUTH BEACH —
2ND WEEK OF MAY 1877.
FROM FACE OF FRONT BUFFER BEAM
TO ₵ FRONT AXLE = 4'-10"
RAIL TO TOP OF PLT = 3'-9"
₵ CYLS TO ₵ DRIVING AXLE
= 7'-10"

GT. YARMOUTH & STALHAM LIGHT RAILWAY. FOX, WALKER LOCOMOTIVE No. 1, TYPE B1. — ORMESBY.

THE FIRST TO RUN BETWEEN YARMOUTH & STALHAM.

1877. Transporting it to Beach station provided the inhabitants with some excellent entertainment. The job was begun at daylight on the Tuesday and two lengths of track were used, one being leap-frogged as it was released by the passage on *Ormesby* over it, in front of the other. Four heavy draught horses provided the tractive effort and the route chosen was up Regent Street, over the Market Place, and along Saint Nicholas Road to the new station. The worst hazard apparently was the corner from Regent Street into the Market Place, but after this was cleared no further trouble was met and *Ormesby* was railed safely on its permanent track during the Wednesday afternoon. As a brilliant spectacle it has never been beaten by any official occurrence, but then, those were more exciting times! All was repeated on 10th July following, when it was the turn of *Stalham* to provide and fulfil the title rôle.

Opposite page: Fig. 1 **General arrangement of Fox, Walker 0-6-0STs *Ormesby* and *Stalham*.**

Plate 1 **Fox, Walker 0-6-0ST *Ormesby*, now renumbered 15, at Yarmouth Beach, with a new boiler and recently repainted, c1899.**

In *Plate 1* we have a view of *Ormesby* after being numbered 15. Quite recently, a boiler drawing for these two engines has been discovered, from which it has been possible to prepare the coloured replica shown in *Fig. 2*. Following are the main dimensions:

Barrel	3ft 5$\frac{1}{4}$in
Barrel, front	3ft 4$\frac{1}{4}$in
Barrel, between tubeplates	8ft 3$\frac{1}{2}$in
Firebox – inside length	2ft 4$\frac{5}{8}$in
Firebox – length outside	3ft
Firebox – width at bottom	2ft 11in
Firebox – width at top	2ft 10in
Firebox – height	4ft 4in
Tubes	114 x 1$\frac{3}{4}$in O/D x 8ft 6in long
Dome	1ft 8in O/D x 1ft 9in high
Smokebox, upper radius	2ft 0$\frac{5}{8}$in
Smokebox, length	1ft 10in
Smokebox, width at bottom	4ft 2in
Heating surface – tubes	410sq ft
Heating surface – firebox	48.5sq ft
Heating surface – total	458.5sq ft
Grate area	7sq ft
Base of foundation ring to CL of barrel	3ft 9in
Base of foundation ring to underside of barrel	2ft 0$\frac{3}{8}$in
Plates (thickness) shell and outer firebox	$\frac{1}{2}$in
Plates (thickness) firebox tubeplate	$\frac{13}{16}$in
Plates (thickness) smokebox	$\frac{3}{4}$in
Length overall over smokebox handles and regulator	14ft 1in
Height overall to top of safety valve lever	8ft 6$\frac{5}{8}$in
Width overall	4ft 2in
Screwed stays	$\frac{7}{8}$in dia. x 4in pitch, all
Rivets	$\frac{3}{4}$in dia. @ 2in pitch
Firehole	1ft 1$\frac{3}{4}$in x 11$\frac{3}{8}$in
Working pressure.	140psi

Plate 2 Fox, Walker 0-6-0ST *Stalham,* having become No. 16A.

These engines possessed several interesting features. The laminated springs were compensated, reversing lever on the right hand side, the valve rods were cranked to clear the front axle and the inlet ports were as straight as possible, giving free steaming as in the shunters two decades later. The steam dome and safety valve were arranged in tandem one over the other. A gusset plate either side braced the front tubeplate to the shell, a feature not always found in locomotive type boilers. A plunger feed pump was mounted on the right hand side but gave an amount of trouble as they could only function when the engine was moving. It was later removed and another injector fitted, thus providing dual feed when required.

Messrs Fox, Walker had a charming stencil used on all their drawings and this unusual item is included here.

Upon the formation of the E&MR these two locomotives were numbered, with *Ormesby* becoming No.15 and *Stalham* No.16. Later, c1905 *Stalham* was awarded the suffix A thus becoming 16A as seen in *Plate 2. Ormesby* No.15 was sold in 1900 to South Hetton Colliery, thus following the Colne Valley & Halstead Railway's (CV&HR) precedent of selling an engine "up north".

In later life *Stalham* was colloquially nicknamed "Black Bess" after it had been transferred to Melton Constable and used as the works shunter in either 1900 or 1901, and *Plate 3* illustrates it in its final form.

Both engines had a hard life. In fact two replacement boilers were delivered, being invoiced on 24th August 1894. One was sent complete with all fittings and mountings, the other plain and without. Bearing in mind the high percentage of salinity in Yarmouth water of that period (I believe it is improved now), 17 years was good going under such conditions. The first rails had been laid during March 1877 and on Monday 6th August that year Major General Hutchinson RE made a thorough inspection of the line and fittings in company with Wilkinson and Jarvis the contractors and Mr Nicholson, the Company secretary. Being obviously the very model of a modern major general he expressed his entire satisfaction with all he had seen, examined and inspected. The next day, 7th August he issued his Certificate of Worthiness. All was now clear for the first opening and service train to depart, dignified and stately, at 6.45am on Wednesday 8th August. Wisely, the Company did not spend much on a meritorious display but the engine – *Ormesby* – and the guard's van were decorated with flowers. The carriages were made by the

Birmingham Waggon Company costing £281 each and a contemporary eye-witness stated the first class compartments were elegantly decorated in "crimson and blue cloth work, with white and gold ventilating roofs". All the staff were experienced men in their profession, and Mr Brown, Superintendent, was ex-GER. The witness continued, "Having tried the new line, we can say that the train proceeded along it swiftly and smoothly and we hope the day is not far distant when we shall be able to extend our acquaintance with North Norfolk by a trip to Stalham by what will then be the Yarmouth & Stalham Railway".

Plate 3 Stalham **in its final form at Melton Constable in 1928, where it was known as "Black Bess".**

At the commencement this local service was as follows:

Yarmouth depart, 6.45am, 10am, 12.45pm, 4pm (Wednesdays and Saturdays only), 5.45pm and 7.30pm. Sunday, 9.15am, 2.30pm and 7.45pm.

Ormesby depart, 7.25am, 9.15am, 10.45am, 2.45pm, 4.37pm (Wednesdays and Saturdays only), 6.30pm and 8.15pm. Sundays 10.25am, 3.15pm and 8.15pm. All trains were Parliamentary with fares at 1d a mile third and 2d first class.

This working required both engines in steam, one for passenger and one for goods. One would be in steam on alternate Sundays leaving the other free for mudding out and any other maintenance jobs as were found necessary. Tough work for the running-shed men and fitters.

At Melton both engines were painted black and lined with a broad cream band in the centre of which was a narrow black strip. Originally on the GY&SLR they were a darkish green with the coupling rods red.

It is not surprising therefore to record that by the end of April 1893 *Ormesby* had logged no less than 209,549 miles. *Stalham* managed 178,975 miles by the end of the same month. They had then recently had "heavy firebox repairs, new half fireboxes etc". *Stalham* was finally scrapped in 1937.

After such worthy service I am sure the directors never begrudged those replacement boilers!

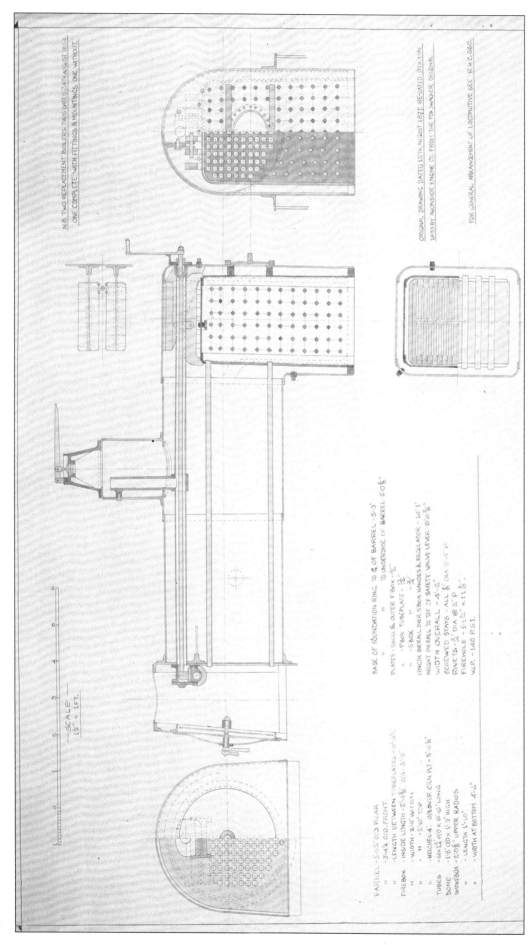

Fig. 2 **Replacement boilers for** *Ormesby* **and** *Stalham.*

14

II

The Tynesiders

IT SOON became apparent that extra locomotive power had become a necessity and so an order was placed with Messrs Black, Hawthorn & Co. for three saddle tank engines similar to *Ormesby* and *Stalham*. Thus at the end of 1877 *Ida* was conveyed to the GY&SLR, builder's number 416 and numbered 7 by the railway. In 1881 two more followed, *Holt,* Black, Hawthorn No. 503 and *Aylsham,* Black, Hawthorn No. 517, but went to the L&FR then progressing eastwards towards Melton and not immediately numbered. Eventually Nos 6 and 7 respectively were allotted by the E&MR.

Holt was subsequently named *Chairman* for obvious reasons but *Ida* was originally named after the Chairman's daughter. One can only hope the young

Plate 4 **Black, Hawthorn 0-6-0ST** *Aylsham,* **having become No. 17A.**

lady appreciated the compliment!

A short history of the builders is very interesting. One John Coulthard commenced building locomotive engines as early as 1835 in his Quarry Field Works, Gateshead. By 1865 he had constructed about twenty for several railways including the York, Newcastle & Berwick, the Blyth & Tyne, the Earl of Durham's Collieries and so on. John had started in partnership with Ralph his brother but the association was dissolved in April 1853 and the firm became R. Coulthard & Co. Ralph retired in 1865 and in this year William Black and Thomas Hawthorn acquired the business and work was concentrated mainly on industrial locomotives. One engine was even sent to Japan! In 1896 Black, Hawthorn & Co. ceased business after making more than 1,100 locomotives and the firm was purchased by Chapman & Furneaux who constructed a further 70 engines, their last being an 0-4-0ST in 1902 builder's number 1215, when they too ceased production and the goodwill, patterns and drawings were bought by R. & W. Hawthorn, Leslie & Co. Ltd. of Newcastle upon Tyne.

The trio of *Ida*, *Holt* and *Aylsham* were, with several small differences, repeats of the Fox, Walker design and in fact *Fig. 1* represents the Newcastle engines very closely. The minor differences were:

Cylinders	14in x 20in
Driving wheels, dia.	3ft 4½in
Wheelbase, leading to driving	5ft 3½in
Wheelbase, driving to trailing	5ft 6in
Wheelbase, total	10ft 9½in
Boiler barrel, dia.	3ft 8¼in
Firebox, height	4ft 7in
Heating surface, total	556.5 sq ft
Height to CL of boiler above rails	5ft 4½in
Height to top of chimney above rails	11ft 2in
Tank capacity	665gall
Fuel capacity	1ton
Weight in W.O.	26ton
Tractive effort @ 80%	10,800lb

The reader will note how closely the two makes agree, so much so that one might be forgiven for imagining that a profuse amount of copying went on between the many builders at this period. In fact normal interchanging of personnel provided the spreading of ideas and so similarities were bound to occur. The slight increase in heating surface of the new engines would be necessary to deal with the extra steam needed for the 14in cylinders as opposed to the Fox, Walker 13in. With decreased driving wheel diameter and an increase of $21\frac{1}{4}$ square inches in piston area the Black, Hawthorns had 10,800lb as against 8,907lb of the Bristol machines.

After *Ida* was delivered she did an amount of work towards completing the GY&SLR into Stalham and was so used by the contractors. By 1881 the line was now the Yarmouth & North Norfolk Railway (Y&NNR) and *Aylsham* was received by the contractors completing the line. Incidentally, upon numbers being allotted, ie *Ida* No. 7, *Holt* No. 6 and *Aylsham* No. 17 by the E&M, the nicely cast nameplates were removed.

According to several sources, the original colour of these early saddle tanks was eggshell black lined with a white edging to a vermilion centre. However, some years ago the late Wilfred Peckett told me it was quite likely they could have been finished in a dark shade of green.

All these engines coursed about Norfolk very well, *Ida* having covered 230,507 miles by the end of April 1893, *Holt* 191,221 and *Aylsham* 200,564 by the same date. *Aylsham's* extra mileage was accounted for by having worked more passenger trains as soon as the link-up was made to Melton, this now providing the through route from South Lynn to Yarmouth. The following year 6 and 7 became 6A and 7A and 17, 17A. In 1894 or 1895, Nos 6A and 7A were sold to the Ibstock Brick & Tile Company through Messrs T. W. Ward.

Apparently, Leicestershire suited them because 7A *Ida* lasted until 1928 with 6A *Holt* reaching AD 1940 ere it went to the scrapyard.

Old *Aylsham*, having become 17A as we have seen, was kept as Melton Constable works shunter and is seen in *Plate 4*. It was not replaced until 1901, being survived by its seven cousins admired in another chapter.

III

Alpha & Vici
The Capable Twins

THESE TWO small contractor's engines were built and supplied by Hudswell, Clarke & Rodgers, Railway Foundry, Leeds to Wilkinson & Jarvis, the same contractors who had constructed the first line for the Great Yarmouth & Stalham Light Railway, but in this instance for the making of the Lynn & Fakenham Railway (L&FR) eastwards and towards Melton Constable. *Fig. 3* shows a general arrangement drawing applicable to both engines.

Alpha bore the manufacturer's No. 183 and was dated 5th October 1878 and *Vici* No. 192 and dated 8th December 1880. Later, after completion of the line, and as Wilkinson & Jarvis had shares in the enterprise, they were taken into the Lynn & Fakenham stock in 1881 and were numbered 4 and 5 respectively. They still carried their names as they did until they were scrapped, the plates being fixed to the sides of the saddle tanks. After the formation of the Joint in 1893, the following year saw them transferred to the Engineer's Department. Here Mr Marriott used them on the building of the direct line to South Lynn and also on construction of the Norfolk & Suffolk Joint line and in the Mundesley area.

Plate 5 **Hudswell, Clarke & Rodgers 0-4-0ST *Alpha* at work in Holt Cutting, 1903.**

The important details and dimension were as follows:

Cylinders	8in x 15in
Driving wheels, dia.	2ft 6in
Wheelbase	5ft
Boiler barrel, dia.	2ft 3in
Boiler barrel length	7ft
Boiler barrel length between tubeplates	7ft 2½in
Tubes – No. x O/D.	39 x 2in
Firebox width	2ft 6½in
Firebox length	2ft 3$\frac{3}{16}$in
Firebox height	3ft 4in
Grate area	5.76sq ft
Heating surface, tubes	186.87 sq ft
Heating surface, firebox	38.15sq ft
Heating surface, total	225.02sq ft
Working pressure	140psi
Rail to CL of barrel	4ft 8in
Rail to CL of buffers	3ft 2in
Buffer centres	5ft 10in
Length over buffers	17ft 8in
Rail to top of chimney	9ft 7in
Chimney diameters	7in to 9in
Chimney, length	3ft 6in
Fuel capacity	7½cwt
Tank capacity	260gall
Weight in W.O.	11ton 10cwt
Tractive effort @ 80%	3,584lb
Frames	14ft long x $\frac{5}{8}$in thick

Plate 6 **Right hand side view of *Alpha* showing feed pipes.**

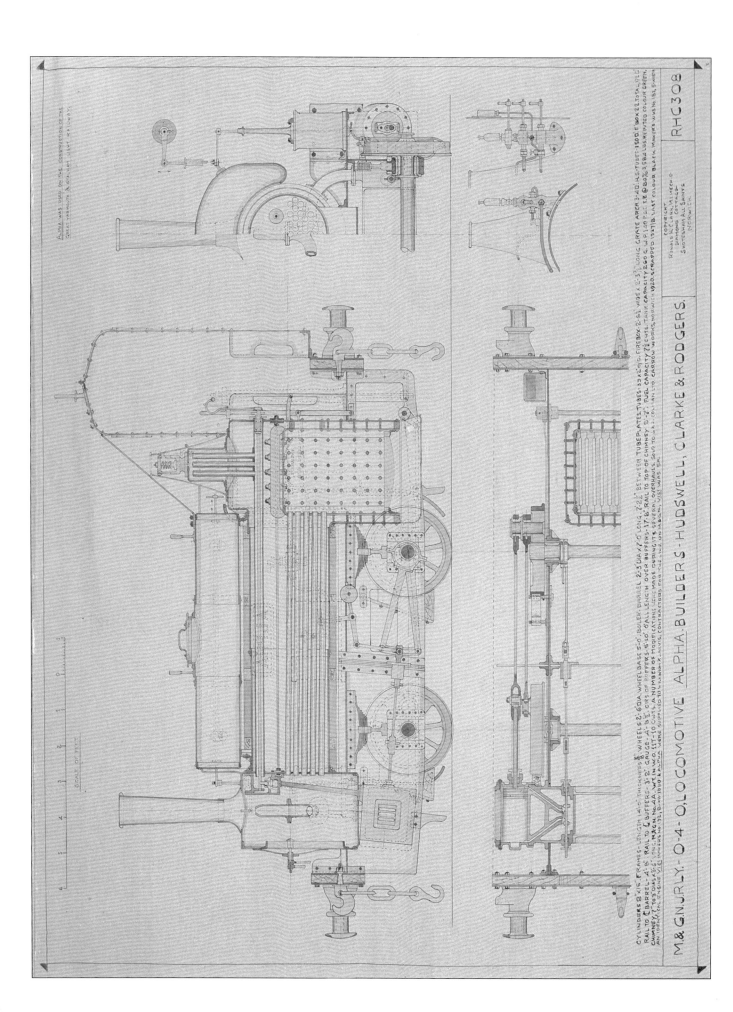

M.& G.N.JT.RLY.- O-4- O. LOCOMOTIVE ALPHA. BUILDERS - HUDSWELL, CLARKE & RODGERS.

RHC 308

SCALE OF FEET

When new it is reputed they were painted a restrained green and probably unlined as shown in *Plate 5*. Nevertheless they were kept very clean and in good mechanical order when owned by the contractors. For a time during and after completion of the line they were used on a certain amount of traffic duty additional to contracting work. Upon absorption into the Joint stock c1881 they were given the numbers 4 and 5, later 4A and 5A, the numbers being fixed to the chimneys with the suffix beneath.

Some further interesting items are worth noting. The brake blocks were of hardwood, oak or poplar. Each locomotive had a pump and injector when new, the pumps being inside the frames, but after such a lapse of time I have been unable to ascertain the exact details of these pumps and the eccentric drive. Later however the pumps were removed and the feed was then by two injectors, as illustrated in the offside view in *Plate 6*.

Vici at one time was used in the construction of spacious brickyard sidings at Dogsthorpe near Peterborough. On this job it was shedded at the latter place. Later it returned to Melton and acted as one of the general purpose engines for works and yards.

In 1917 *Alpha* was properly reconditioned, painted black and lined in gold and sold to Messrs J. & J. Colman Ltd., Carrow Works, Norwich. It was used to handle their heavy yard traffic and is seen in its new livery ready for delivery to Norwich in *Plate 7*. Some time afterwards several parts were required and as *Vici* was nearing scrapping, these were cannibalised from 5A, thus leaving it partly dismantled and by 1929 it was looking very derelict.

At that time the author was on the engineering maintenance staff at Carrow Works and well remembers little *Alpha* at work. For some now unaccountable reason I had the urge to collect all the known details relating to this engine from the chief engineer's office and these have proved of inestimable help and value in preparing *Fig. 3* and compiling these notes. *Alpha* was eventually scrapped in 1928 being replaced by a new Peckett 0-4-0 saddle tank locomotive. To cope with the increasing shunting, a Barclay 0-4-0 Fireless

Opposite page: Fig. 3 **General arrangement of Hudswell, Clarke & Rodgers 0-4-0STs** *Alpha* **and** *Vici*.

Fig. 4 **Details of Hudswell, Clarke's chimneys.**

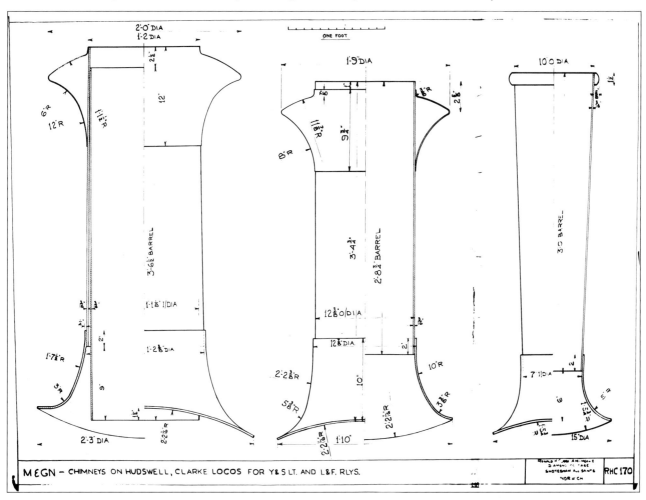

M£GN – CHIMNEYS ON HUDSWELL, CLARKE LOCOS FOR Y&S LT. AND L&F. RLYS.

locomotive was later purchased new and both worked contentedly for some years.

Alpha and *Vici* had raised fireboxes as depicted in *Fig. 3* with three vertical collecting pipes, typical of the maker's practice, to ensure dry steam into the main tube to the regulator. The appendage on the cab roof was a lamp bracket to carry a four spectacle white light.

This was obviously highly necessary when working in dark and dull conditions moving ballast wagons surrounded by labourers, as when building a new line. A good example of "safety at work" we hear so much about today. Operation of the sanding gear was by a rod through each handrail and the details in *Fig. 3* will make the method clear.

During the 1920s an evening train left Norwich City for Drayton, calling at Hellesdon. On one occasion the booked train engine failed due to tube trouble and the only locomotive engine available was *Vici*. Mr Alan Wells told me his father was the driver who had quite a hard time forcing the train along with only 2ft 6in driving wheels! However it reached Drayton, ran round its train and completed the return journey to Norwich. The travelling public in those days must not be let down.

On a visit to the builder's works no drawings of these small engines were to be found, only a sketch of the chimneys was discovered. Nevertheless from data lent to me I have been able to prepare *Fig. 4* and the chimney details of all the firm's locomotives supplied to Norfolk aided by the information previously mentioned from Carrow Works. When at Leeds it was suggested I investigate the old estimating and costing books preserved in an upper room "over the stables". To my great joy I disinterred some dusty piles of thick, leather-backed books wherein I discovered the costing of these small saddle tanks, together with the costings appertaining to the 4-4-0 tank engines dealt with elsewhere.

Plate 7 Alpha **as reconditioned in 1917 for Messrs J. & J. Colman Ltd, Carrow Works, Norwich.**

The costings for *Alpha* and *Vici* were as follows:

	£	s	d
Boiler	85	2	7
Framing	31	17	0
Coke boxes	10	1	8
Tank	7	5	9
Iron castings	23	14	0
Brass castings, etc.	12	17	6
Mountings	16	16	2
Sundries	27	17	2
Motion	23	14	2
Copper work	17	10	4
Wheels	25	19	6
Total	£282	15 s	10 d

Carriage on 5th October 1878 by Midland Railway Co. to Lynn was 9 tons at 17s 3d per ton = £7 15s 3d. *Vici* however, having a few small differences, cost £286 10s 9d. The carriage on 8th December 1880 by GNR was 9½ tons at 20s 6d per ton = £9 14s 9d. The cost sheet also bears the interesting statement "Carriage to Fakenham Town". How *Vici* was moved from the GER station to the L&F line, then building at the other side of the town, I have not yet discovered. It could have been leap-frogged on three lengths of rails, as was done at Yarmouth and North Walsham, or alternatively a temporary spur may have been laid from the existing GER line as mentioned in the Act of 1876.

The reader may wonder at the reference to "stables" in a locomotive

Plate 8 Alpha **at work on building the Mundesley branch.**

manufactory. In the heyday of Leeds locomotive manufacturing a team of horses was kept on a co-operative basis, supported by all the Leeds locomotive builders, these elegant creatures being used to haul new engines to the nearest railway siding if there was no siding to any works. In the case of Messrs Thomas Green & Sons new engines were pulled on their flanges, along the length of a neighbouring street to the nearest siding of the Midland Railway. Leeds Corporation turned a blind eye as maintenance of employment in the city was paramount.

A final view of *Alpha* at work making part of the Mundesley branch is included in *Plate 8*. It looks a real working engine doing a useful job of work, unlike so many over-painted and restored "glass case" examples often seen to-day.

IV

The Seven Sisters

AS WE HAVE observed already the Y&NNR was worked by the only three locomotives they possessed viz *Ormesby, Stalham* and later *Ida*. But as both goods and passenger patronage increased, extra engine power became very necessary. To achieve this the Company ordered three graceful looking 4-4-0 side tank engines from Hudswell, Clarke & Rodgers, builder's numbers 208, 210 and 232 and named respectively *North Walsham*, *Martham* and *Great Yarmouth*. Curiously, they were delivered in no set order apparently, because No. 208 arrived 9th September 1879, 210 on 24th May the same year and 232 on 31st October 1881.

After the Y&NNR had become absorbed into the L&FR this latter company ordered four more of the same design and to simplify names and builder's numbers, these details are given in the following table:

Builder's No.	Delivered	Ordered by	Name	Co. Nos	Joint Nos	Withdrawn
208	9-9-78	Y&NNR	*North Walsham*	E&M 32	41	c1904
210	24-5-79	Y&NNR	*Martham*	E&M 31	40	?
232	31-10-81	Y&NNR	*Great Yarmouth*	Y&NN 19	19	1917
209	6-11-78	L&FR	*Hillington*	E&M 8	8	May 1917
211	20-6-79	L&FR	*Fakenham*	E&M 9	9	1932
231	3-10-81	L&FR	*King's Lynn*	E&M 20	20	Oct 1932
224	28-10-80	L&FR	*Norwich*	E&M 10	10	May 1917

Note that most appropriately they were named after Norfolk towns and villages. As mentioned they were very elegant little engines as one will see from *Plate 9* being an ex-works photograph of North Walsham and the only one to be found at Leeds. They all left that city painted a medium green. On some the lining was a wide band of vermilion unedged. On others the lining was black and white lines outside the vermilion band, the frames being a medium brown.

They all had interesting lives. For example in 1906 the Joint loaned to the Midland Railway (MR) Nos 8, 10, 19 and 40 where they were used for "push & pull" services. In exchange the Joint received three MR 0-4-4 side tank engines, their numbers 141-143, for six years. When used on the MR rail motor services they were coupled to old Pullman cars which had come from the USA, as long ago as 1874. The locomotives were attached bunker end to the car and in one direction the driver had to be at the front end of the car

Plate 9 Hudswell, Clarke & Rodgers 4-4-0T *North Walsham*, from an official works photograph.

and he made communication with his fireman by means of an endless rope. One end was connected to a dummy regulator in the driving compartment and the other to the regulator proper on the engine. For notching up he had a ship's telegraph system installed with a dial at the end of the car to suit facing the end of the bunker where it could be seen by the fireman who altered the lever as indicated, upon receiving the driver's instructions. Needless to say vacuum brake fittings were duplicated in the car driving department. *Plate 10* shows one of this class attached to a Pullman car at Harpenden.

For some years on this service the four engines retained their M&GN livery but the MR crest was placed on the side tanks in the centre in place of the M&GN letters. Their numbers were altered to correspond with the car numbers so that No. 8 *Hillington* became No. 2, No. 10 *Norwich* became No. 5, No. 19 *Great Yarmouth* became No. 1 and No. 40, *Martham* became No. 10.

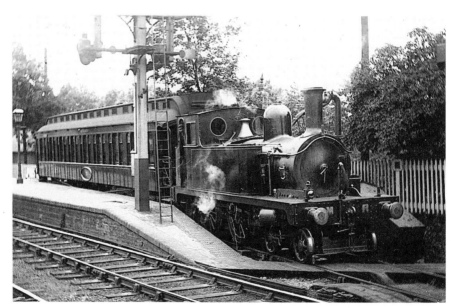

Plate 10 One of the "Seven Sisters" and a Pullman car in use as a rail motor at Harpenden, Herts, whilst on loan to the Midland Railway.

By 1908 Nos 8 and 40 were rebuilt at Derby and No. 10 a little later. In *Plate 11* we have a view of No. 10 after rebuilding when its number, it will be noticed, is in plain white numerals. All three were returned to the M&GN replete with Midland parallel engine chimneys, but unchanged otherwise. It was while they were away that Nos 9 and 20 became 9A and 20A in 1909. The main duty of No 9A was to work the Engineer's and Director's Saloon at Melton at this period but often the work was shared with No. 20 and a delightful view of the latter attached to this saloon is to be enjoyed in *Plate 12*. Also, both handled much of the local traffic between Bourne and Saxby and between Melton and Norwich City. Early in the First World War the four lent to the MR were sold to the Government and went to Forant, Bordon, Rhyl and Ormiston Colliery. One or two were used for re-railing exercises etc.

Following are the main dimensions of *North Walsham* and *Hillington:*

Cylinders	14in x 20in
Wheels, dia. bogie	2ft 4in
	later 2ft 5½in
Wheels dia driving	4ft 6in
	later 4ft 7½in
Wheelbase bogie	4ft 10in
Wheelbase bogie centre to leading driving	8ft 3½in
Wheelbase, driving	6ft 9in
Wheelbase, total	17ft 5½in
Barrel, dia	3ft 7in
Length between tubeplates	9ft 6½in
Firebox – length	3ft 6$\frac{9}{16}$in
Firebox – width	3ft 8in
Tubes – No. x dia.	100 x 1¾in
Heating surface, tubes	512.6sq ft
Heating surface, firebox	53.2sq ft
Heating surface, total	565.8sq ft
Grate area	9sq ft
Working pressure	140psi
Tank capacity	750gall
	later 835gall
Fuel capacity	17cwt
	later 25cwt
Rail to underside of footplate	4ft 2in
Rail to CL of buffers	3ft 4in
Rail to top of chimney	12ft
Length over buffers	27ft 9in
Weight in W.O.	34ton
Weight on bogies	11ton
Weight on driving axle	12ton
Weight on trailing axle	11ton
Weight total	34ton
Tractive effort @ 80%	8,130lb

There were slight differences embodied in *Martham* and *Fakenham,* however where the cylinders were finished 15in x 20in, the grate area increased to 11 sq ft as against 9 for the first pair. The extra heating surface of 623 sq ft was provided to produce more steam for the 15in cylinders. In turn this increased the tractive effort to 9,333lb instead of 8,130lb. Increasing the barrel diameters slightly enabled the boilermakers to fit in 15 extra tubes. Concerning the wheels, it was quite common practice to increase the first diameter upon re-tyring, thus allowing for re-turning by stages back to the original diameter. In the case

Plate 11 Ex-Lynn & Fakenham Railway 4-4-0T No. 10 after rebuilding.

Plate 12 A 4-4-0T, probably No. 20, attached to the Inspection Saloon.

of *Great Yarmouth*, *Norwich* and *King's Lynn* the small boiler alterations enabled the overall heating surface to be increased as above and including *Martham* and *Fakenham*. But exactly what these small boiler modifications were has not been ascertained.

All wheel centres were of wrought iron and the bogie truck of the swing bolster type. An unusual item on *North Walsham* were the covers to the crosshead guides, probably necessary when working along the coast just north of Yarmouth. Some were later removed. No pumps were fitted, the feed relying

on two injectors feeding to the front ring of the barrel. The connecting rods
were forked at the little ends with the cross-head body working within the
fork, and closed type big-ends with long bearings on the pins. They worked
outside the coupling rods. Springing was by underhung springs, those in the
bogie being inverted in the cradle. The sand boxes were incorporated in the
front bottom parts of the side tanks, the brake blocks were of suitable hardwood, and the bulb lubricators on the smokebox supplied both cylinders and
steam chests. Later Roscoe pattern lubricators were substituted. Safety-valve
bases, chimney cap, and domes were of polished brass, as were the side window
frames, and these, together with the graceful curves incorporated in the outline of the cab, gave the engine most attractive lines. It is remarkable however
that no cylinder drain cocks were fitted by the makers and it ran for 26 years
without trouble.

When visiting the upper room recounted in the history of *Alpha* and *Vici*
I also discovered the cost sheets of these seven locomotives and the details
for Nos 231 and 232, *King's Lynn* and *Fakenham* were as follows:

	£	s	d
Boilers	481	14	5
Framing	206	0	5
Coke, boxes, covering etc.	38	0	3
Tanks	47	4	2
Iron castings	119	3	1
Brass castings	99	18	1
Mountings	49	13	5
Sundries	98	2	7
Motion	88	9	2
Copper work etc.	84	19	5
Axles, wheels and springs	213	17	10
Bogies	96	1	4
Total	£1,623	4 s	2 d
Total, each	£811	12s	1d

Plate 13 **The author's favourite of the "Seven Sisters", No. 19, formerly Y&NNR *Great Yarmouth*.**

29

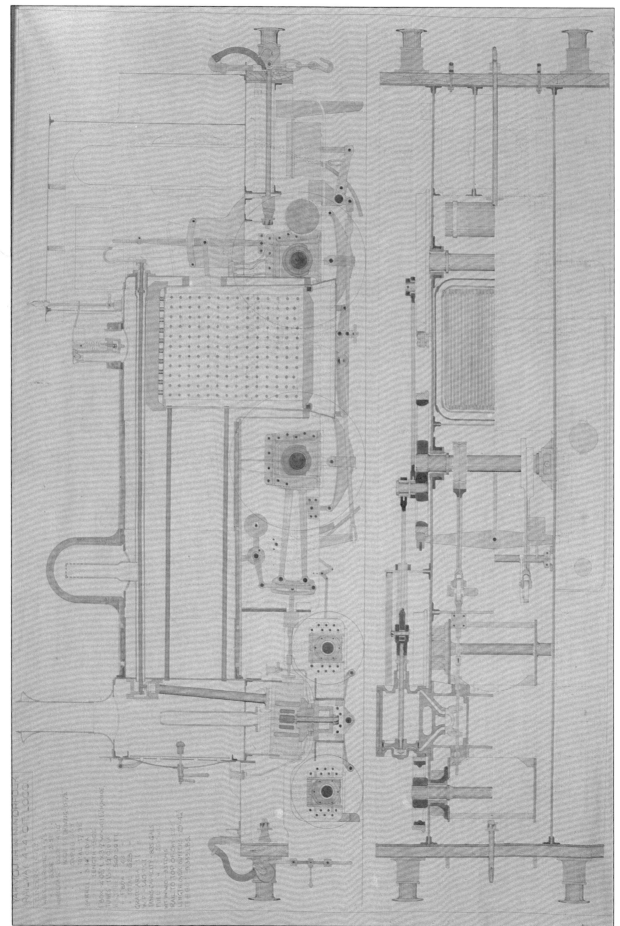

Fig. 5 General arrangement of Hudswell, Clarke & Rodgers 4-4-0Ts.

Transport costs too are interesting. The carriage of 3rd October 1881 (No. 231) to Lynn (MR), 26 tons at 17s 3d = £22 8s 6d. Carriage 31st October 1881 (No. 232) to North Walsham (GNR), 26 tons at 20s 10d = £27 1s 8d. Similarly, *Norwich* (No. 224) cost £823 15s 7d the carriage to Lynn by the MR being 26 tons at 17s 3d = £22 8s 6d.

Incidentally the preserved delivery note for No. 211 *Fakenham* specified it was to be delivered on 20th June 1879 to our old friend Daniel Crowe of Gaywood. *Fakenham* was required to open the primary section of the line to Great Massingham.

The remaining details of the design can be studied in the coloured drawing in *Fig. 5*. My favourite of these Seven Sisters was *Great Yarmouth*, No. 19 to be seen in *Plate 13*.

Once again there was the problem of final delivery when in the case of *North Walsham* it was delivered on the dock side on 9th September 1878 and caused some greater difficulty during its journey through the streets due to its weight being about eight tons heavier than the Bristol Rovers. *Martham* reached its permanent track by the same means. However my favourite, No. 19 arrived at North Walsham GER station and road snag-hauled to the L&FR station.

Of course locomotives had to be paid for and for the half year ending 31st December 1880 the Y&NN paid the builders £559 3s 3d, which was charged to the Company's capital account. In the two half years of 1881 it paid out £600 and £200 respectively, after which it appears all engines now delivered and possessed had been paid for with no deferred payments outstanding.

Hudswell, Clarke & Rodgers became a world-famous concern who made and sent locomotive engines all over the world. Three founders were involved, James Kitson, the son of mine host of the Brunswick Tavern in North Leeds, Charles Todd, who had served his time with the great Matthew Murray and David Laird, a wealthy Scots farmer who provided some much needed financial support. This triumvirate acquired a small plot of land in Pearson Street and erected what they called the Railway Foundry. They were successful from the start by booking an order for six engines for the Liverpool & Manchester Railway, the first two bearing the names *Lion* and *Tiger*, cylinders 12in x 18in 0-4-2 wheel arrangement and delivered in 1838 costing, £1,100 each. *Lion* became world famous and appeared in two films, *Victoria The Great* and *The Titfield Thunderbolt*.

Apparently these three individuals failed to work too well together because Kitson and Laird moved to other premises to form the Airedale Foundry. After their departure Todd was joined by one John Shepherd and so the firm became Shepherd & Todd. In 1840 they were supplying locomotive engines to the York & North Midland and the Hull & Selby railways. In 1843 Matthew Murray's famous concern Fenton, Murray & Jackson closed, and many of their employees found work with Shepherd & Todd. One ingenious young man, David Joy, also had to find other work and as an apprentice he finished his time by moving to the Railway Foundry. Again there was a break in the partnership with Todd's precipitate departure in June 1844. However by that time, about twenty engines had been built. In his place came one Edward Brown Wilson, the son of a Hull family of shipowners, who moved into the Railway Foundry in November 1844. After only six months he shrewdly appointed the young David Joy to the position of Acting Chief Draughtsman.

Another break occurred in 1846 with Wilson leaving the firm, but, as it happened, only temporarily. His locum was James, son of James Fenton of the former Fenton, Murray & Wood, aided by an ex-pupil of the Railway Foundry viz John Chester Craven. November 1846 saw them come up with the new title Fenton & Craven. As many readers may know Fenton & Craven made the famous *Jenny Lind*, 2-2-2 tender locomotive with the "Long" boiler and 15in x 20in cylinders. Fenton now became works manager but Craven left to join the Brighton Works. Thus the company was now styled E. B. Wilson & Co., the plain contemporary work's plate proclaiming "Railway Foundry Leeds".

To cope with ever increasing orders Wilson needed to expand and he managed to purchase or lease all the land of the Pearson Estate nigh unto the existing small works. No time was lost and the new erecting shop was completed by June 1848. Owing to a shortage of income the last two locomotives from the Railway Foundry proper were completed in 1858 when the firm closed down.

In July 1859 the buildings and plant were sold by auction, but a plot of land on the west side of Jack Lane, having an area of 7,283 square yards (1.505 acres) was acquired by private purchase by two engineers, William Shillito Hudswell and John Clarke. There was a third partner, Dr William Clayton, a Leeds surgeon but he was mainly a sleeping partner. Thus the new name "Hudswell & Clarke, Engineers" appeared on the site of the old Railway Foundry, the name of the works being continued. This new concern started building locomotives on 1st December 1860.

Plate 14 **4-4-0T No. 40 at North Walsham on a through train to Yarmouth.**

Plate 15 **One of the 4-4-0Ts, probably No. 19, on the Engineer's Saloon in the vicinity of Roughton village.**

Now in 1866 one Joseph Rodgers joined the firm as a director but the enormous success of his pulleys, based on his Patent No. 3389 of 1866, induced the partners to add his name to the firm's title and thus we get the "Hudswell, Clarke & Rodgers" on the early nameplates.

One final change took place in 1883 when Rodgers, not apparently a very popular character, being a self-made man, severed his connection when the firm took its last title " Hudswell, Clarke & Co, Railway Foundry, Leeds", with the simple telegraphic address "Loco. Leeds".

Small wonder then that with such a long industrial history and ancestry, the Seven Sisters proved hard-working characters combined with such dainty and elegant outlines. Not only was No. 20 used to haul the inspector's saloon but No. 9 also performed this duty at various times.

Plate 16 **A ballast train headed by either No. 19 or 20A, between Stalham and Ormesby.**

For small engines this class certainly ran up a goodly score in mileage because by the end of April 1893 their totals were: No. 8 – 214,944. No. 9 – 225,103. No. 10 – 275,421. No. 19 – 342,247. No. 20 – 308,247. No. 31 – 363,771. No. 32 (renumbered 41 in 1886), – 320,501.

As my reader has undoubtedly gathered, the "Seven Sisters" were used in the early days of the L&FR and later by the Joint on a variety of work and *Plate 14* depicts No. 40 on a through train for Yarmouth in North Walsham station, complete with the appropriate head code. Note the neatly trimmed box shrubs and the most substantial footbridge.

For a time No. 19 was taken off its usual Melton-Yarmouth-Norwich route and used on inspection workings during the construction of the Cromer-Mundesley line, and the front end view in *Plate 15* shows such an occasion, probably in a new cutting in the area of Roughton village.

It was not often that any of the "Seven Sisters" were rostered for goods duties but fortunately I am able to record such an occasion in *Plate 16*. The working appears to cover a ballast train somewhere in the flat lands between Stalham and Ormesby. The locomotive could be No. 19 or 20A but not improved in looks by the bare stovepipe chimney.

The works' records tell me that when new they were painted a dark green, single lined with deep yellow. From their chief draughtsman I also learned that the design for these locomotives was evolved entirely by their own drawing office and attributive to no other source.

V

The Cornish Derivatives

TO SERVE many Cornish tin and coal mines and china clay workings the Cornwall Minerals Railway (CMR) was established by an Act of Incorporation dated 1873, with its main line commencing at Fowey and extending westwards through Par, Bugle, Roche and finally terminating at Newquay. Branch lines ran in from Treamble to Tolcarn Junction near Newquay, from Melangoose Moor, Burngallow and finally a short spur from Carbis. Most of the lines were open by 1st June 1874. Co-existing was the Cornish Railway running from Bodmin Road, through Par, Saint Austell and on to Truro. This introduction is of necessity rather brief, as apart from the foregoing, little is relevant to East Anglia.

Unfortunately the traffic hoped for failed to materialise which resulted in the undertaking being taken over by the GWR on 1st July 1877. That company then worked the traffic from 1st July of that year onwards, receiving 53% of the gross receipts. The GWR, now the working company, found they could dispose of nine of the 18 special 0-6-0 tank engines built by Sharp, Stewart & Co. in 1874 for the CMR, these being numbered 1-18 in the CMR list. This disposal was as follows: nine locomotives kept by the GWR and one to the Colne Valley & Halstead Railway (CV&HR), all in 1877. Three were returned to Sharp, Stewart & Co. and re-sold to the Lynn & Fakenham Railway in 1880 and five were also re-sold to the E&MR in 1882.

The odd one out was No. 10 on the CMR list. At this period, 1880, Mr J.W. Mann, in charge of rolling stock on the L&F inspected five of these engines, ostensibly for the CV&HR. In reality of course his inspection was mainly on behalf of the L&F but he "worked in" this odd example to oblige. As a result the CV&HR acquired No. 10 builder's No. 2358, this small company's lack of funds precluding their buying more than one engine. Plate 17 shows No. 10 as supplied to the CV&HR at Halstead, and painted dark green. That Mr John Crabtree, recently appointed general manager of the railway was a friend of Mr J.W. Mann, trained under Edward Fletcher of the NER and of Mr William Marriott, may have had some influence on the deal. Upon coming to Halstead it was named *Haverhill* and the Chairman of the Company was Mr W. Bailey Hawkins who simultaneously was chairman of the South Hetton Colliery. This explains how when *Haverhill* was sold in 1889, now with an all-over cab, it went to the above colliery! Major Elyot S. Hawkins, son of Mr Bailey Hawkins, later became the last manager of the CV&HR and was a friend of my grandfather's, the late Walter Clark of Halstead. Perhaps this may account for my making several trips as a student, firing No. 5, the Hudswell, Clarke 0-6-2T goods engine during a summer vacation many years ago. After sale to South Hetton Colliery they gave it their No. 21 additional

Plate 17 Cornwall Minerals Railway 0-6-0T
No. 10, as later sent to the Colne Valley &
Halstead Railway in Essex.

to the two *Haverhill* nameplates. Here it worked until 1948, an amazing tribute to Francis Trevithick whose designs for these small engines were made
initially on behalf of Sharp, Stewart. Incidentally the *Haverhill* nameplates are
now preserved in the H.Q. of the Stephenson Locomotive Society.

On the CMR they were intended to work "back to back" in pairs with
just a curved weatherboard for protection but one solo is to be seen in *Plate
18* being CMR No. 15. After complete reconditioning as found necessary by
Sharp, Stewart, one finished engine has been shown in *Plate 17* being No. 10
on the CV&HR and those sent to Norfolk being described as identical. As
no authentic photograph has been found, this Essex locomotive is included
as being representative of the re-sold series. According to the builder's records
all were finished in a medium green and had full cabs added by them before
delivery to Norfolk. It is not now known for certain the route traversed by
these engines to Norfolk, but they were delivered via the GER to Gaywood
Sidings on the Lynn-Hunstanton line. All motion work would of course be
disconnected and the locomotives hauled as a heavy vehicle in the appropriate train. It is interesting to note that Daniel Crowe of Gaywood Sidings started
in c1860 a blacksmith's and wheelwright's shop, later expanded, and close to
the Lynn-Hunstanton main road and near the crossing of it over the GER
line. By 1867 he had built a self-moving threshing machine and later a three-
wheeled traction engine and in 1868 formed his business into the Gaywood
Agricultural Company with him remaining very much in charge. No better
place than to send an engine to be un-loaded and steamed for the first time
after its arrival. An admirer of the Monarchy, he called his small establish-

Plate 18 Sharp, Stewart 0-6-0T No. 15 of
the CMR in its original state. It later
became L&FR/E&MR No. 3 *Blakeney.*

ment the Victoria Steam Works. We meet with him again later.

At this point the following table will clarify the dates and numbering which took place:-

L&FR and E&MR No. and name	Builder's No.	Date Built	CMR No.	Date Acquired	Cost £
1 *Melton Constable*	2372	1873/4	17	1880	?
2 *Reepham*	2371	1873/4	16	1880	?
3 *Blakeney*	2370	1873/4	15	1880	?
11	2360	1874	11	1881	1,200
12	2361	1874	12	1881	1,200
13	2368	1874	13	1881	1,200
14	2369	1874	14	1881	1,200
18	2373	1874	18	1881	1,200

Those delivered as tank engines only, as in *Plate 18,* were numbers 1, 2 and 3. Tenders were supplied by the builders in 1881 with Nos 11 – 18 being supplied as tank engines but with builder's tenders fitted, as depicted in *Plate 19.* One interesting feature of No. 17 (L&FR No. 1) was the addition of a full length cab with a backsheet for better weather protection, but all the others had cabs only as received from the Atlas Works, Great Bridgewater Street, Manchester.

The main dimensions of these interesting little engines were as follows:

Cylinders	$16\frac{1}{4}$ x 20in
Wheels, dia.	3ft 6in Later 3ft $7\frac{1}{2}$in
Boiler barrel O/D	4ft $0\frac{3}{8}$in
Boiler length between tubeplates	8ft 2in
Boiler shell plate	$\frac{7}{16}$in thick
Boiler tubes O/D	195 x $1\frac{3}{4}$in
Firebox inside width	3ft $4\frac{1}{8}$in
Firebox inside length	3ft 3in
Firebox inside height	5ft 2in
Grate area	10.82sq ft
Heating surface, tubes	752.8sq ft
Heating surface, firebox	70.7sq ft
Heating surface, total	823.5sq ft
Working pressure	140psi
Wheelbase – leading to driving	5ft
Wheelbase driving to trailing	6ft
Wheelbase total	11ft
Height to top of chimney	12ft 6in
Height to CL of boiler	6ft 1in
Height to CL of buffers	3ft 3in
Top of running plate	3ft $9\frac{1}{2}$in
Buffers, CL	5ft 9in
Weight in W.O. leading wheels	10ton 7cwt
Weight in W.O. driving wheels	10ton 17cwt
Weight in W.O. trailing wheels	9ton 12cwt
Weight in W.O. total	30ton 16cwt
Weight empty	24ton 10cwt
Fuel capacity	15cwt
Fuel consumption on passenger work	28lb per mile
Water capacity	780gall
Load on goods work	30 sheeted wagons
Tonnage	300tons
Overall length	30ft $5\frac{7}{8}$in
Overall width	8ft 6in
Tractive effort @ 80% W.P.	14,030lb
Left hand crank led in fore-gear.	

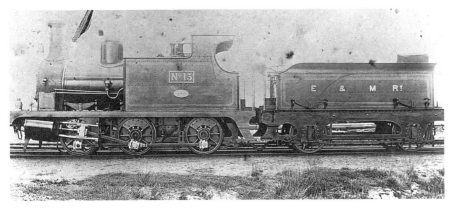

These particulars should be studied in conjunction with the coloured drawings in *Fig. 6*. Melton painted them chocolate lined in black and yellow.

Note the boilers had raised firebox crowns like *Alpha* and *Vici*, and these were the only locomotives on the Joint to have this feature. Steam domes had detachable tops giving easy access to the regulator valve and rod. As built they all had screw reversing gear, but later at Melton Constable, they were converted to lever operation. Originally the brakeblocks were of hardwood used endwise to the grain, but later cast iron was substituted. When the L&FR became merged into the Eastern & Midlands Railway the names of the first three were removed. No. 13 however was fitted with a Westinghouse pump.

Withdrawal dates of these small engines were as follows: No. 1 – 1898, No. 2 – 1894, Nos 3 and 11 – 1899, No. 12 – 1902, No. 13 – 1898, No. 14 – 1897 and No. 18 – 1895. Nos 1 and 2 were for tax purposes, classed as "rebuilds" but were apparently scrapped. However many parts were used later on as described in another chapter. Recorded mileages at withdrawal were: No. 1 – 244,471, No. 2 – 228,051, No. 3 – 235,961, No. 11 – 236,872, No. 12 – 190,753, No. 13 – 237,609, No. 14 – 236,410 and No. 18 – 244,176.

The reader will easily appreciate that with driving wheels only 3ft 6in or 3ft $7\frac{1}{2}$in in diameter it could be hard work keeping time on the long single stretches prevalent on the Norfolk lines. To remedy this Mr William Marriott, Chief Engineer at Melton Constable, had carried out a "metamorphosis" or great change to four of this class, the altered engines being No. 18 in 1890 and Nos 3, 13 and 14 spread over 1891/2 when they became 2-4-0 tender locomotives. *Fig. 8* shows an engraving emanating from the works' preserved records and this, along with the delightful photograph in *Plate 20*, will make the design quite clear – bearing in mind some details not too apparent in one illustration are augmented in the other.

To achieve this change the frames were cut out an extra $2\frac{1}{2}$in making the footplate 4ft above rail level, and a strengthening Low Moor iron plate was riveted inside. Fresh cast steel driving wheels of 4ft 7in diameter were obtained from the builders, these being one of their standard parts used for other and industrial locomotives. In design they were very similar to Worsdell's creation, which he used on certain engines. The leading wheels were retained but with new horncheeks and brass boxes with wrought iron tops permitting some lateral play. The driving boxes were also of brass with adjustable wedges. Both side tanks were removed with splashers and sand boxes substituted. Obviously some adhesive weight was lost but this was compensated for by fitting Holt & Gresham's sanding gear. Clackboxes were placed at the firebox end and a Vacuum Oil Company's sight feed lubricator put on the right hand side of the cab. The engine footplate having been raised $2\frac{1}{2}$in as we have noticed, and now that amount above the tender plate, a baulk of suitable timber was placed to bring the two footplates level. It is interesting to note however that a difference in level can be seen in the case of No. 18 in *Plate 20*. The original Stephenson gear was changed to Allen straight link gear, designed specially for this application. It must be remembered that all this creditable work was carried out in the Melton shops and drawing office.

Another view, this time of No. 13 gracefully adorning the turntable, is to be seen in *Plate 21* where several odd diversions will be noticed when compared with the details of No. 18.

These tenders were of simple design as will be noted from the various

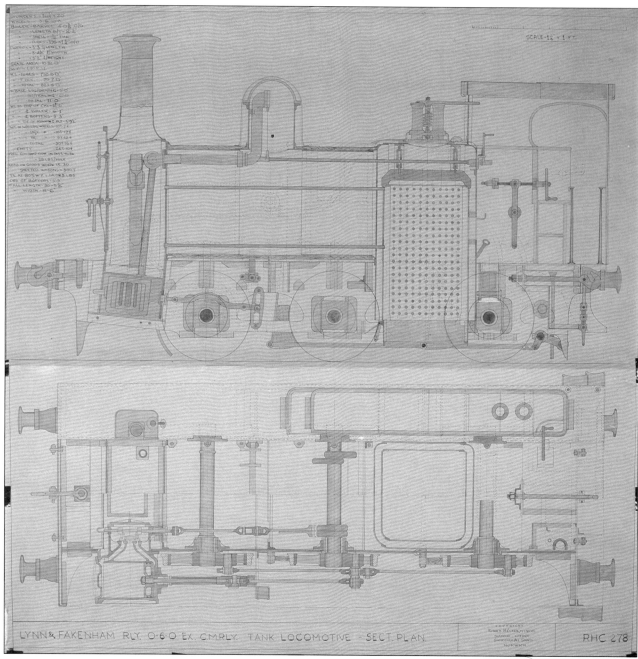

LYNN & FAKENHAM RLY. 0-6-0 EX. C.M.R.LY. TANK LOCOMOTIVE - SECT. PLAN.

RHC 278

Fig. 6 **General arrangement of a Cornwall Minerals Railways 0-6-0T.**

Opposite page: Fig. 7 **General arrangement of the Sharp, Stewart tenders for ex-CMR locomotives.**

illustrations, and also from the coloured drawings in *Fig. 7.* Following are the main dimensions:

Overall length	18ft 7in
Overall width over footplate	7ft 2in
Overall width over cab footplate	8ft 8in
Overall width between frames	6ft
Overall width over water tank	5ft 4in
Wheels, dia.	3ft 6in
Wheelbase	9ft 6in
Height of original running plate above rail	3ft 9½in
Height of above when timber baulk provided	4ft
Tank capacity	1,150gall
Coal capacity	3ton
Weight in working order	15ton 10cwt
Total weight, engine and tender	45ton
Tractive effort @ 80%	10,392lb
Painting: a medium chocolate brown	

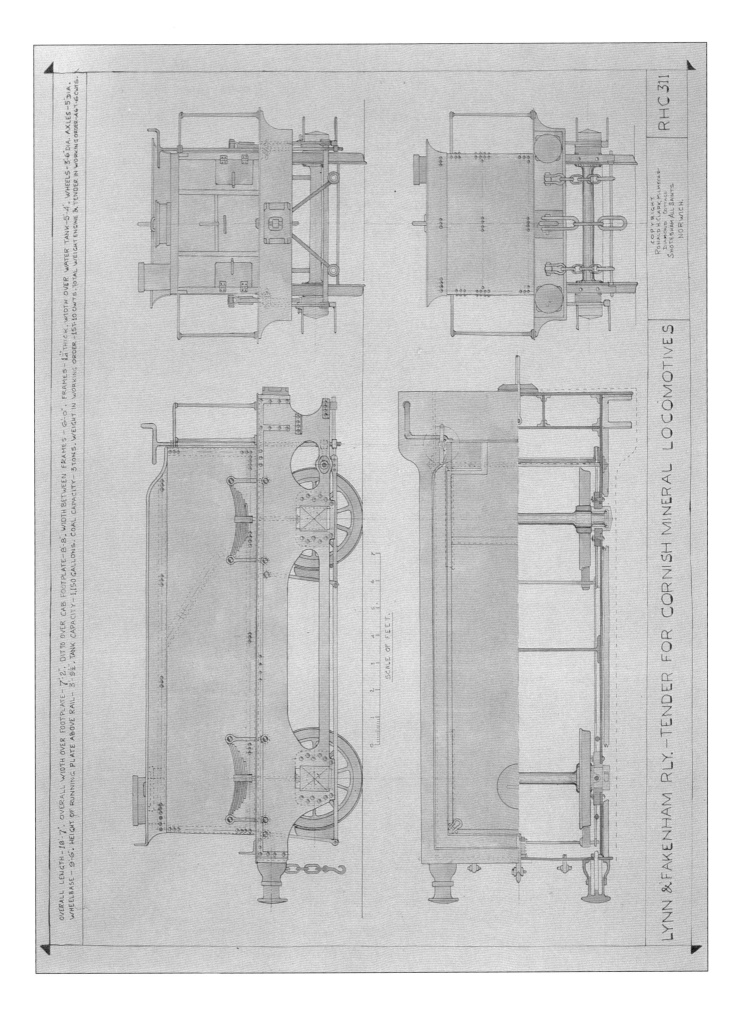

OVERALL LENGTH - 18'-7'. OVERALL WIDTH OVER FOOTPLATE - 7'-2'. DITTO OVER CAB FOOTPLATE - 8'-8'. WIDTH BETWEEN FRAMES - 6'-0'. FRAMES - ½" THICK. WIDTH OVER WATER TANK - 5'-4'. WHEELS - 3'-6" DIA. AXLES - 5" DIA. WHEELBASE - 9'-6'. HEIGHT OF RUNNING PLATE ABOVE RAIL - 3'-9½'. TANK CAPACITY - 1,150 GALLONS. COAL CAPACITY - 3 TONS. WEIGHT IN WORKING ORDER - 15T-10 CWTS. TOTAL WEIGHT ENGINE & TENDER IN WORKING ORDER - 45T-16 CWTS.

SCALE OF FEET.

LYNN & FAKENHAM RLY.—TENDER FOR CORNISH MINERAL LOCOMOTIVES

RHC 311

Fig. 8 **A contemporary engraving of CMR 0-6-0T No. 14.**

Plate 20 **Former Cornwall Minerals Railway, Sharp, Stewart 0-6-0T No. 18 after rebuilding to a 2-4-0 tender locomotive in 1890.**

As one can imagine there are always detractors from another man's work and it was so in this case. Several incompetents prophesied the boilers would generate only enough steam for the Westinghouse pump. Quite baseless, as if the boilers steamed well when first received, they would obviously steam as well again! Proof is to be seen in *Plate 22* where No. 13 is shown dealing with a goods train of average load at Martham. What I think gave rise to these adverse comments is that some drivers had not appreciated the difference in performances was due to the reduction in tractive effort, viz about 3,600 pounds. If of course a good fireman kept the needle on the red mark there would be

Plate 21 **E&MR 2-4-0 No. 13 posed on a turntable.**

a small increase in drawbar pull due to a slight increase on the calculated 80% of the working pressure on the pistons, and so the driver would obtain a marginally better performance.

Long after this series of engines had been scrapped several of their tenders survived, having been converted to mobile fresh water tanks for supplying water, mainly for staff domestic and similar purposes at out-of-the-way localities. One or more existed even until the 1960s! The last engine to survive was No. 12, having been transferred to Yarmouth Beach and used on the construction of the Norfolk & Suffolk Joint line from there to Lowestoft.

One amusing anecdote is recorded about No. 11. Its driver "Lumpy" Ling had reported a faulty regulator. Now Ling, having left the engine for a short spell when at South Lynn, was shocked to see it quietly and gracefully moving off on its own and unattended. He sprinted to the best of his ability but managed only to touch one buffer. The line was cleared for a "runaway" and having by its own peaceful efforts become short of steam, it ambled into Hillington station. As the late Mr William Newman told me, one of the station staff boarded her, applied the handbrake with no little assiduity and stopped just short of the crossing gates!

Plate 22 **2-4-0 No. 13 on a goods train at Martham.**

VI

The Nine Brothers

AS THE DERIVED Cornish Minerals engines were scrapped there arose the inevitable shortage of small shunting locomotives as at this period c1900, there were only six saddle and side tank examples available. To replace those scrapped or sold away Mr Marriott conceived the idea of producing an MR type side tank, six-coupled class suitable mainly for shunting and also for short haul goods and passenger services when necessary.

In order that due economy was observed he used as many items and fittings as possible from the scrapped units, mainly wheels, several pairs of linered cylinders, some motion gear and so on. New boilers were used, coming mainly from Derby Works and whereas the CMR boilers had a barrel 4ft $0\frac{3}{8}$ in O/D the new had barrels with a mean diameter of 3ft 10in outside x 4ft 3in diameter over the lagging. The new frames were cut for wheelbases of 6ft 3in and 7ft 6in respectively. *Fig. 9* shows details of these boilers and was made from a drawing dated 1900 with the main dimensions being as follows:

Barrel, max O/D	3ft 11in
Barrel, min. O/D	3ft 9in
Barrel, shell plate	$\frac{1}{2}$in thick
Barrel, length between tubeplates	9ft $11\frac{5}{8}$in
Firebox, length inside	3ft $6\frac{7}{8}$in
Firebox, width inside	3ft 2in
Firebox, height inside	4ft 8in
Tubes O/D	145 x $1\frac{3}{4}$in
Heating surface, tubes	670sq ft
Heating surface, tubes firebox	67sq ft
Heating surface, total	737sq ft
Grate area	11.35sq ft
Length overall	14ft $8\frac{1}{4}$in
Width overall	4ft
Height to top of firebox crown	6ft 2in
Designed W.P.	160psi
Actual W.P.	140psi

The main difference was the flat firebox crown, unlike the raised crown in the Cornish engines, fewer tubes and less total heating surface. Otherwise there was little deviation from the Sharp, Stewart proportions found in *Fig. 6,* as will be seen from the other following main dimensions:

Cylinders	16in x 20in
Driving wheels, dia.	3ft 6½in
Wheelbase, leading to driving	6ft 3in
Wheelbase, driving to trailing	7ft 6in
Wheelbase, total	13ft 9in
Height to CL buffers above rail	3ft 5in
Height to CL boiler above rail	6ft 4¾in
Height to top of chimney above rail	11ft 9½in
Height to top of cab roof above rail	11ft 2½in
Overall length, approx.	32ft
Weight in W.O. leading axle	11ton 2cwt 3qr
Weight in W.O. driving axle	14ton 2cwt
Weight in W.O. trailing axle	11ton 19cwt
Weight in W.O. total	37ton 13cwt 3qrs
Coal capacity	1½ ton
Water capacity	800gall
Tractive effort 80% W.P.	13,493lb

Although the cylinders were reduced to 16in diameter, the decrease in piston area was only 6.33 sq in giving a reduction in load of 709lb thus keeping the tractive effort to within a few hundred pounds of the original Cornish engines. In the odd cases where original cylinders were used they were linered down to 16in bore. The new cylinders are detailed in *Fig.10* which illustrates a right hand cylinder. All had inlet ports as straight as possible to aid free steam flow, in short a very neat design and thermodynamically good. The CMR wheels had ten spokes rectangular in cross-section whereas the replacement wheels had twelve spokes elliptical in cross-section. Thus the source of wheels is easily established. *Plate 23* shows No.1A where it will be noticed the connecting rods are outside the coupling rods and have open-ended big-ends with the small-ends adjusted by screw and wedge.

These delightful little engines were produced at Melton Constable in the following order: Nos 3A and 14A – 1887, No. 1A – 1898, No. 11A – 1899, No 15 – c1900, Nos 12A and 17A – 1902, No. 2A – 1903 and No. 16 – 1905. Shortly after the last was constructed the duplicate listed engines were renumbered 93-99 in 1907. Thus No.3A became 95 but 15 and 16 retained these numbers. Other details are, chimneys of the third Melton pattern, MR boiler fittings and mountings, and a fountain just forward of the spectacle plate from which steam for the whistle and other fittings was drawn. There were steam brakes to driving and trailing wheels and a handbrake with vertical spindle. In

Plate 23 M&GN 0-6-0T No. 1A.

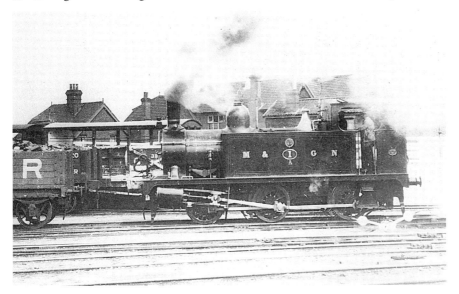

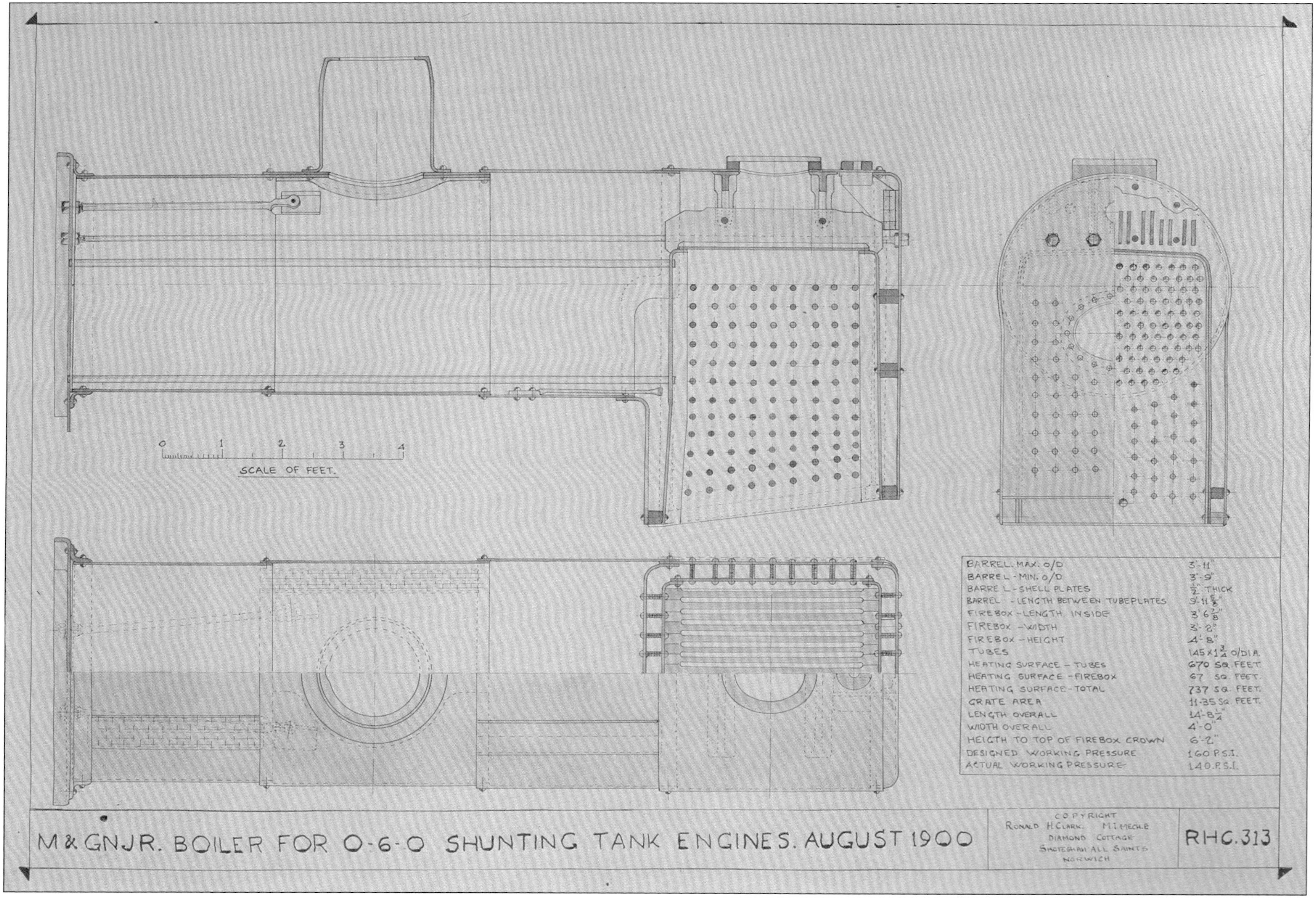

BARREL MAX. O/D	3'.11"
BARREL MIN. O/D	3'.9"
BARREL L. SHELL PLATES	$\frac{1}{2}$" THICK
BARREL LENGTH BETWEEN TUBEPLATES	9'.11.5"
FIREBOX LENGTH INSIDE	3'.6.5"
FIREBOX WIDTH	3'.2"
FIREBOX HEIGHT	4'.8"
TUBES	145 x 1$\frac{3}{4}$" O/DIA
HEATING SURFACE TUBES	670 SQ.FEET.
HEATING SURFACE FIREBOX	67 SQ.FEET.
HEATING SURFACE TOTAL	737 SQ.FEET.
GRATE AREA	11.35 SQ.FEET.
LENGTH OVERALL	14'.8.5"
WIDTH OVERALL	4'.0"
HEIGHT TO TOP OF FIREBOX CROWN	6'.2"
DESIGNED WORKING PRESSURE	160 P.S.I.
ACTUAL WORKING PRESSURE	140 P.S.I.

SCALE OF FEET.

0 1 2 3 4

M & G N JR. BOILER FOR 0·6·0 SHUNTING TANK ENGINES. AUGUST 1900

COPYRIGHT
RONALD H. CLARK. M.I.MECH.E
DIAMOND COTTAGE
SMEETHAM ALL SAINTS
NORWICH

RHC.313

Fig. 9 The boiler for the **Melton** built 0-6-0Ts.

Plate 24 M&GN 0-6-0T No. 97 in Norwich City goods yard, 1937.

Plate 25 Official photograph of M&GN 0-6-0T No. 3A, later No. 95.

particular the injectors were fitted below the tanks for flooding if they should not start at once and get overheated, a position usually adopted by the traction engine makers for the same reason. To anyone who has had to cajole a hot injector to function, this advantage needs no labouring! Also included were bulb type lubricators, vacuum brake pipes and sanding gear for running in either direction. *Plate 24* illustrates No. 97 hard at work in Norwich City goods yard in 1937. Note the extra fuel hopper fitted centrally on top of the bunker, adding a further half ton. These were added c1930 as I remember clearly, No. 98 shunting in South Lynn yards 1929/30. It would be No. 97 too which I saw and admired so often in Norwich yards and even once at Drayton, and in its original state.

A retired driver, Marshall Cartwright of South Lynn, told me that after hoppers were fitted he could work all day on South Lynn – King's Lynn shuttle passenger services on one full load of coal at his morning start. These locomotives had a long life and their withdrawal dates were No. 93 – July 1945,

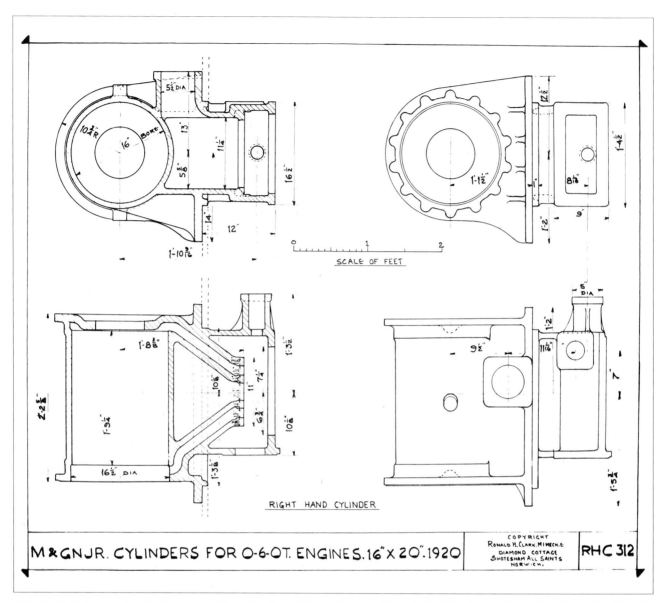

M&GNJR. CYLINDERS FOR O-6-OT. ENGINES. 16"X 20". 1920

Fig. 10 **Cylinder drawing for the nine M&GN 0-6-0Ts.**

No. 94 – Jan. 1948, No. 95 – Dec. 1947, No. 96 – May 1948, No. 97 – March 1943, No. 98 – Jan. 1947, No. 99 – July 1945, No. 15 – Dec. 1945 and No. 16 – Aug. 1949.

Plate 25 is a works' photograph of No. 3A, later 95, which illustrates clearly how all this class appeared when new. The late Mr William Newman told me several covered 65,000 miles between light overhauls in Melton shops. Incidentally it is most interesting to note the oval plate on this locomotive reads:-

M & G N
REBUILT
1897
MELTON CONSTABLE

(Some authorities have given the dates as 1899. However I prefer to believe the plate in this case!)

To finish this chapter I think the action picture in *Plate 26* of No. 98, dealing with some of the 1912 flood damage at Norwich City, is most appropriate.

Plate 26 0-6-0T No. 98 on flood damage repairs at Norwich in 1912.

VII

Nos 42 and 43 –
The Lancastrians

SHORTLY AFTER the Eastern & Midlands Railway had been formed by the amalgamation of all the lines East of Lynn in 1883, this company bought in November that year two 2-4-0 mixed traffic engines from the LNWR and originally built for the Lancaster & Carlisle Railway. Mr Marriott, who had been superintendent and resident engineer in charge of the building of the connecting link between Melton Constable and North Walsham, knew Francis Webb at Crewe very well, and it was because of this connection that the E&MR were able to purchase these two extra locomotives. Both engines had been built in 1857 by Rothwell, Hick & Rothwell, at the Union Foundry, in Bolton for the Lancaster & Carlisle Railway.

To simplify the rather involved numbering and re-numbering of these engines recorded later, I feel a few notes on the L&CR at this juncture would be helpful. The railway was authorised in 1844, the existing Grand Junction Railway subscribing £250,000 in support. The Act provided for a single line, 70 miles long with Joseph Locke as engineer. His route lay over Shap Fell, rising to 900ft up 1 in 75 for approximately five miles. Locke's contractors were McKenzie, Stephenson & Co. who made such excellent progress that the line was opened through to Carlisle on 17th December 1846. There was now a complete link between London and Carlisle via Rugby, Birmingham, Warrington, Preston and Lancaster.

Simultaneously the Caledonian Railway had obtained an Act in 1845 for their main line joining Glasgow with Carlisle. Making excellent progress the 9,615 men and 99 horses completed their task so that this line was opened in 1848. Therefore there was a complete route linking London with Glasgow, including the Caledonian branch to Edinburgh, with the L&CR now forming a very important portion.

Another development occurred in 1852 when the Midland Railway leased a portion of the line of the LNWR, connecting Skipton with the L&CR at Lancaster. This route proved to be somewhat circuitous, so in 1857 the L&CR obtained Parliamentary powers for a direct and new line joining Low Gill on its own line, to Ingleton, where there was a branch of the LNWR. It was opened in 1861. Now previously, in 1859 the LNWR had taken over a lease of the L&CR for 999 years. It proved a wise move as the former company now had control of the complete route from London to Carlisle, a distance of 300 miles. It was over this hard route up and down Shap Fell that the original L&CR 2-4-0s had to work both goods and passenger trains.

To return to the two engines which came to the E&MR. They were two of a set of 20 bearing the builder's numbers 158 to 177. Their L&CR numbers were 1–20. The pair that eventually ended up at Melton Constable were

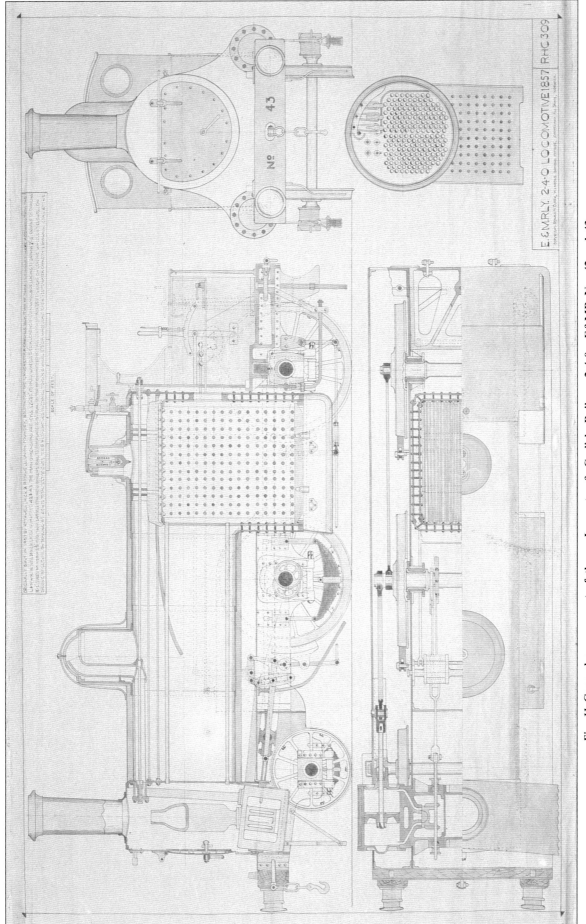

Fig. 11 General arrangement of the ex-Lancaster & Carlisle Railway 2-4-0s, E&MR Nos 42 and 43.

builder's numbers 160 and 165, L&CR Nos 3 *Sedgewick* and 8 *Luck of Edenhall*. After the take-over the LNWR in 1859 *Sedgewick* had become LNWR No. 319 and *Luck of Edenhall* No. 384, both on 22nd December of that year. At Crewe they were transferred to the duplicate list in July 1869 as Nos 1118 and 1802 respectively. However they were returned or restored to the Capital List in December 1871 and re-numbered 1101 and 1112. When sold to the E&MR in November 1883 they had again possessed duplicate numbers 1855 and 1776 respectively. On arrival in Norfolk the E&MR numbered them 29 and 30. Yet another re-numbering took place when the E&MR bestowed upon them their final numbers, viz 42 and 43. Apparently the LNWR had removed their names c1873. Undoubtedly the E&MR got a good deal as a spare frame and wheels for *Luck of Edenhall* were sent to Carlisle running shed during October 1882 and it is pretty certain these had been fitted before the pair of engines had left for East Anglia.

Upon the amalgamation of the L&CR with the LNWR, Francis Webb acquired all the former's locomotives and speedily set about reboilering and rebuilding them as found necessary. They had had a hard life, pounding up and down over Shap Summit for twelve years. As built they had driving wheels 5ft 1in dia. Webb fitted new, extra thick tyres, increasing the diameter to 5ft 2in, a slight increase in top gear ratio may we say. At Melton, Mr Marriott eventually turned them down to their original 5ft 1in. The outside cylinders were 17in x 20in and the slide valves were operated by Allen straight link motion. All the salient features and details can be studied in *Fig. 11*. It must be remembered that all 20 engines went back to the builders at least once during their time with the L&CR, when minor alterations must have been made to bring them up-to-date. Then too, Webb fitted new boilers so that several small fittings have not been recorded, but I believe *Fig. 11* to be as complete and authentic as can be ascertained after such a long lapse of time. The main dimensions are given separately later and they can be studied with reference to the drawing. They were elegant looking engines and typical of their period, as will be seen from the photograph reproduced in *Plate 27*. The new boilers were of Webb's own design and proved very successful, not only on these rebuilt L&CR engines but on other classes on the LNWR.

Plate 27 **Right hand side prospect of ex-Lancaster & Carlisle Railway 2-4-0 No. 8 *Luck of Edenhall* as E&MR No. 43.**

Following are the main dimensions:

Cylinders	17in x 20in
Driving wheels, dia.	5in 1in
Leading wheels, dia.	3ft 2in
Wheelbase, leading to driving	7ft 3in
Wheelbase, driving to trailing	8ft 1in
Wheelbase, total	15ft 4in
Tubes No.	198
O/D	$1\frac{3}{4}$in
Boiler, barrel dia.	4ft
Boiler length between tube plates	9ft 9in
Firebox width	3ft 4in
Firebox length	4ft 8in
Firebox height	5ft $6\frac{1}{2}$in
Heating surface, tubes	884.8sq ft
Heating surface, firebox	103.44sq ft
Heating surface, total	988.25sq ft
Working pressure	140psi
Grate area	15.5sq ft
Rail height to footplate	3ft 9in
Rail height to top of chimney	12ft 8in
Overall length	25ft approx.
Overall width	8ft $1\frac{1}{2}$in
Main axles, dia.	$6\frac{1}{2}$in
Leading axle, dia.	$5\frac{1}{2}$in
Weight on leading wheels	6ton 12cwt
Weight on driving wheels	9ton 14cwt
Weight on trailing wheels	6ton 4cwt
Weight, total	22ton 10cwt

Valve gear: Allen straight link. Reversing on L.H.S.

Plate 28 **Cabside detail of 2-4-0 No. 43A.**

It is said Crewe Works were noted for much hand fitting to its locomotives inasmuch that major parts could be hand fitted to their allotted frames.

As received at Melton Constable they had the four-wheeled McConnell original tenders replaced by a later six-wheeled type with outside springs. These carried 1,800 gallons and three tons of coal. The six wheels were 3ft 9in diameter on a wheelbase of 5ft 6in + 5ft 6in = 11ft. I regret insufficient details have been discovered to make any authentic drawings possible.

A certain amount of rebuilding occurred during their working life at Melton Constable, but exactly what alterations or additions were made is not now known. It is reputed that modifications were made to their cabs and Howe valve gear substituted for the Allen straight link motion, and reversed on the right hand side. Other parts such as the chimneys and brake gear had new parts where found necessary. Both engines had separate hand brakes to both engine and tender as they were not fitted with continuous brake gear. These additions and alterations were made between 1891 and 1893. Their classification was Class C.

It is said No. 42 was broken up at Norwich shed c1895, although this would have proved hard going at a shop without major facilities. No. 43 suffered the same fate at about the same time but more easily one would say, at Melton.

Mileages on the E&MR on 30th April 1893 were No. 42 – 156,649 and No. 43 – 162,357. I have heard it said that neither engine was "very much good", but I feel these mileages contradict any such talk.

Rothwell, Hick & Rothwell was started off by Benjamin Hick in Bolton in c1830 with Rothwell as his partner. However, he left two years later and set up on his own in the same town and business, calling his firm Benjamin Hick & Sons. Rothwell then called his concern Rothwell & Company with Union Foundry as its address. Rothwell, Hick & Rothwell are perhaps best known for building Pearson's then enormous 4-2-4 express locomotive in 1853 for the Bristol & Exeter Railway. Benjamin Hick, incidentally, had spectated at the Rainhill Trials. Altogether about fifty of the 2-4-0s were built. However, owing to the intense competition in the locomotive field at this period, orders fell off from 1856 and after a few more years the firm closed. Part of the works were bought by the Bolton Iron & Steel Company, well known in the railway world. Then, c1907, Henry Bessemer acquired the rest of the property. Altogether about 200 locomotives were built at the Union Foundry, the last being completed in 1864.

The reader may wonder at the name of *Luck of Edenhall*. It is explained by the fact that Eden Hall was the family seat of the Musgrave family and an ancient legend proclaimed that:

> The drinking glass of crystal tall
> They call the Luck of Edenhall;
> Should this goblet break or fall
> Farewell the Luck of Edenhall.

VIII

Parvo Cristátus – The Peacocks

THE BESTOWING of the above title to a class of locomotives arose from what was really a term of affection expressed by drivers, other ranks and many members of the public, familiar with these elegant examples of locomotive beauty. I must say I yielded to no one in my admiration for the class and was always cheered by the sight of one of them. As the ornithological examples also give one great pleasure, I deem the above titles to be neatly appropriate.

Altogether there were 15 of them classified Class A, all built and supplied by Beyer, Peacock & Co. of Manchester and they were delivered under the following circumstances. As early as 1881 the Lynn & Fakenham Railway realised the Seven Sisters were unable to deal adequately with the growing traffic arising from the line, now being continuous from Lynn to Yarmouth. Therefore in 1881 the Company ordered four 4-4-0 tender express engines which were delivered in March 1882 and they were numbered 21-24, bedecked in a refined shade of green. This batch had builder's numbers 2105-8. They proved so successful that four more were ordered by the Lynn & Fakenham, delivered in November 1883, and numbered 25-28, builder's numbers 2338-2341. Numbers 25 and 26 arrived on 14th November and 27 and 28 on the 20th

Plate 29 No. 33, one of the final batch of the "Peacocks", in original condition.

of the same month. By this time the L&FR, had been absorbed into the Eastern & Midlands and so all engines were lettered to suit. All had cost £3,000 each. Later in 1886 three more were ordered and came to Norfolk to be numbered by the E&MR 29-31, builder's numbers 2794, 2795 and 2798, having cost only £2,000 apiece. No. 29 arrived on 2nd November, No. 30 on 12th November and No. 31 on 19th November. Finally the Eastern & Midlands directorate in 1888 ordered a concluding clutch of four and gave them sequence numbers 32-35, as seen in *Plate 29*. Beyer, Peacock's numbers were 2939-2942, but the price had risen to £2,300 each because ejectors and vacuum brake gear were extras. With these 15 new locomotives, the company's haulage power was adequate for the time being and continued so until, as will be noted later, the late 1890s.

The full details of this pleasant design can be studied in the coloured drawing reproduced in *Fig. 12* and from which the main dimensions have been listed as follows:

Cylinders	17in x 24in
Cylinders, horizontal centres	6ft 3in
Travel of valves	6in
Wheels, driving dia.	6ft
Wheels, bogie dia.	3ft
Wheelbase, bogie	6ft 6in
Wheelbase, bogie centres to driving	10ft
Wheelbase, driving	8ft 2in
Wheelbase, total	21ft 5in
Boiler, barrel O/D	4ft 2½in
Boiler, barrel length	10ft 3½in
Boiler, barrel length between tubeplates	10ft 6½in
Firebox – length	5ft
Firebox – width	3ft 6½in
Firebox – height at front	5ft 10in
Firebox – height at rear	5ft 1½in
Grate area	17.7sq ft
Tubes	204 x 1¾in O/D
Heating surface, tubes	988sq ft
Heating surface, firebox	95sq ft
Heating surface, total	1,083sq ft
Working pressure	140psi
Rail to CL of boiler	6ft 10in
Rail to underside of footplate	4ft 0½in
Rail to CL of buffers	3ft 5in
Rail to top of chimney	13ft 2in
Weight on bogies	14ton 0cwt 3qr
Weight on driving	12ton 4cwt
Weight on trailing	12ton 2cwt 2qr
Weight total	38ton 7cwt 1qr
Weight for adhesion	24ton 6cwt 2qr
Width between frames	4ft 2in
Length overall	29ft
Tractive effort @ 80%	10,789lb

As I have mentioned previously, Norfolk water is not kind to boilers and in the coastal and Yarmouth areas, with its additional saline content, particularly so. Therefore it is not surprising that after the almost usual fifteen years or so, No. 21 received a new Midland Railway "C" boiler in 1896, new chimney, new dome and Salter safety valves. My own opinion, shared by many, is that these alterations enhanced the general appearance of the class. To put

it another way, the fledgling peacock had blossomed into its final and adult plumage as seen in the impressive illustration of No. 26 shown in *Plate 30.* The whole class were in various years fitted with this MR type "C" boiler. Full rebuilding also took place in different years, No. 21 in 1914 for example. Further maintenance particulars are given in the following table:

Plate 30 No. 26 in the impressive final form of the Beyer, Peacock 4-4-0s, as matured at Melton Works.

No.	1st new boiler and first rebuild	2nd new boiler and second rebuild	Mileage by 30th April 1893	Withdrawn
21	1896	1914	340,328	1936
22	1898	1915	398,123	1936
23	1895	1919	364,539	2/1937
24	1898	1914	364,162	5/1941
25	1906	1920	312,887	1936
26	1904	1923	348,602	11/1936
27	1905	1927	343,275	2/1937
28	1905	1925	311,686	2/1938
29	1906	?	252,021	1931
30	1906	?	244,412	1933
31	1907	?	206,395	1933
32	1907	?	199,808	1933
33	1908	?	203,767	1936
34	1908	1931	164,707	?
35	1909	?	199,644	1933

Notes:

No. 22 Fitted with MR tender.

No. 23 New boiler fitted at Stratford, 1919.

No. 24 New boiler 1920, cracked frames.

No. 25 New boiler 1924.

No. 26 1923 boiler in 1924.

No. 27 New boiler 1927.

No. 28 1925 boiler in 1937.

No. 35 Scrapped at Melton.

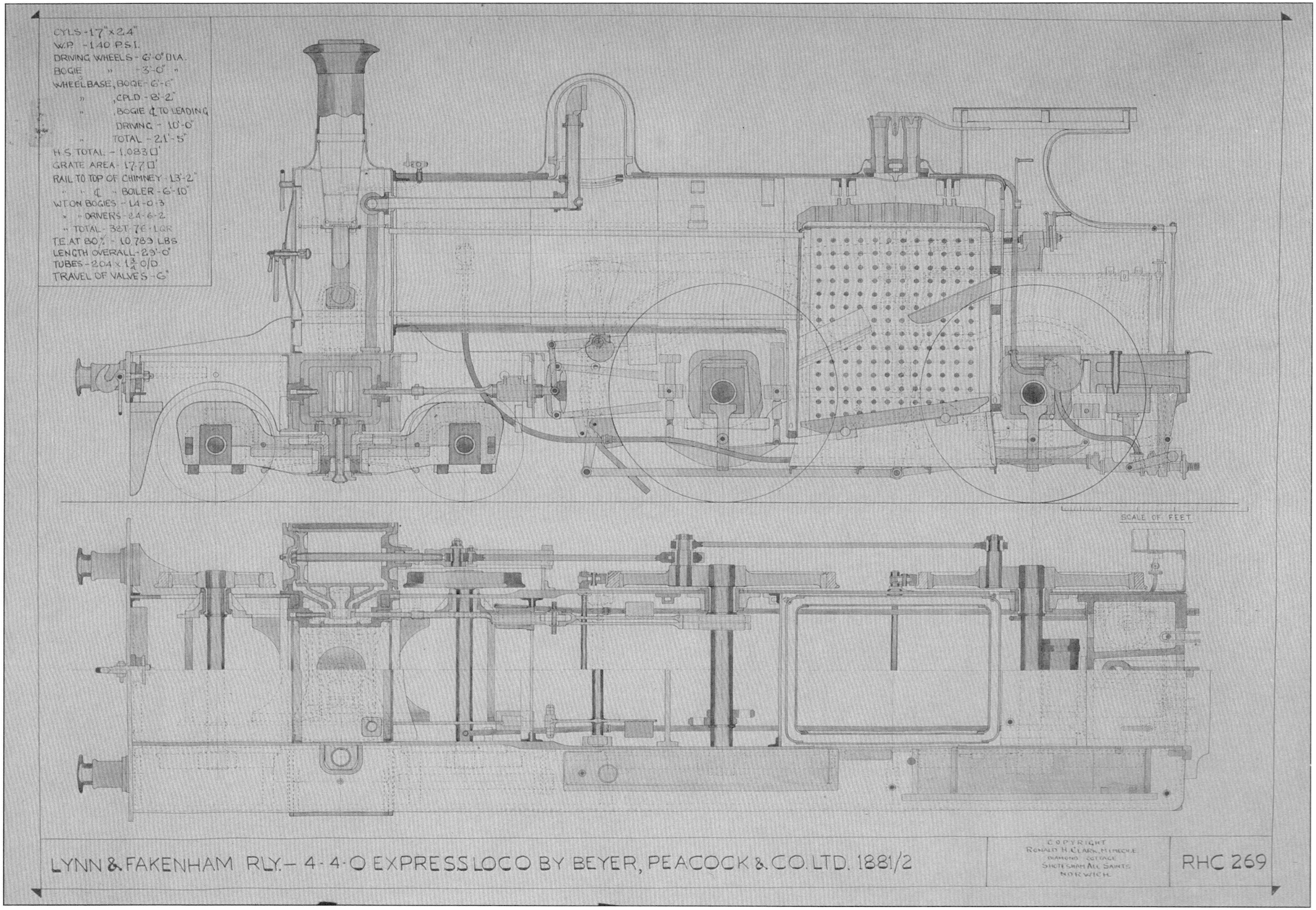

CYLS -17" x 24"
W/P - 140 P.S.I.
DRIVING WHEELS - 6'-0" DIA
BOGIE " - 3'-0"
WHEELBASE, BOGIE - 6'-6"
" , CPLD - 8'-2"
" , BOGIE ℄ TO LEADING
DRIVING - 10'-0"
" TOTAL - 21'-5"
H.S. TOTAL - 1,083 ☐'
GRATE AREA - 17.7 ☐'
RAIL TO TOP OF CHIMNEY - 13'-2"
WT. ON BOGIES - C. - BOILER - 6-10
" - L4-0-3
" - DRIVERS - 24-6-2
" - TOTAL - 35-7-6-10R
T.E. AT 80% - 10,783 LBS
LENGTH OVERALL - 29'-0"
TUBES - 204 x 1¾'' O/D
TRAVEL OF VALVES - 6"

SCALE OF FEET

RHC 269

COPYRIGHT
RONALD H. CLARK AND THEODORE
BOXMORE - GEORGE
SKETCHAM, ALL SAINTS
NORWICH.

LYNN & FAKENHAM RLY.- 4-4-0 EXPRESS LOCO BY BEYER, PEACOCK & CO. LTD. 1881/2

Fig. 12 General arrangement of Beyer, Peacock 4-4-0s Nos 21-35.

From time to time odd and interesting changes during rebuilding and overhauling were carried out in Melton Shops. A classic example concerns Nos 24 and 25. After stripping and detailed examination in 1929 the frames of No. 24 were found to be woefully cracked and the boiler too costly to repair. This did not worry the management at all because No. 24 had the frames and boiler from No. 25 grafted onto its remaining items, No. 25's tender attached and then emerged from the erecting shop proudly displaying "25" on its sides! As Mr W.E. Newman hinted to me, the remaining bits and pieces of the real No. 25 went into stock! Nevertheless, "No. 25" looked resplendent in unlined glossy black. Several others of this class were also operated upon by those Melton mechanics who fitted new cabs, chimneys and straight-sided tenders and the new No. 25 is depicted, after its sympathetic treatment, in *Plate 31*. How the offside appeared is illustrated by *Plate 32* where No. 26 is standing in Cromer yards. Two other unusual views of No. 35 are to be seen in *Plates 33* and *34*, where sad to relate, it was standing on the scrap siding in April 1936. The builder's curved brass nameplate is just visible around the leading splasher. Some lost their plates over the years but all those I saw in traffic were polished until they shone.

Plate 31 Beyer, Peacock 4-4-0 No. 25 after sympathetic modifications by the Melton shops, as LNER No. 025 at Spalding in 1937.

In c1893 the Westinghouse pumps were removed and the Midland Standard steam vacuum brake gear fitted. Another minor detail were the two lifting jacks carried by many of this class, mainly on the later examples as seen clearly in *Plates 29* and *34*, the latter illustration showing precisely the position and method of fixing. Apparently Nos 21-28 had their jacks removed during rebuilding. The usual loading for this type of railway jack was 20 tons.

Until the coming of the Johnsons the Peacocks were always employed upon the more important tasks and still were for many years afterwards. In *Plate 35* we see No. 31 in charge of a repair train on the Blackwater Bridge renewal after the great flood of 1912. In numerous cases they hauled weed-killing trains and a good example is depicted in *Plate 36* but which engine was involved is not now known.

Although the Peacocks ranked as express engines they were often pressed into service for other odd or special jobs. An excellent example is to be seen in *Plate 37* where No. 32 is in charge of the track-laying alterations during the major re-siting of the running lines at the new South Lynn station. Note No. 32 is in its pre-rebuilt form with tall chimney and very high dome.

No. 24 was famous for several special jobs. One, which will appeal to my

Plate 32 Right hand side view of 4-4-0 No. 26 in Cromer yards.

Opposite page: Fig. 13 General arrangement of the tenders for the Beyer, Peacock 4-4-0s.

Plate 33 Upper front view of No. 35 at Melton, April 1936.

sporting readers, was to haul the football excursion on Tuesday 1st September 1908 from Melton to Norwich City. It is fortunate that one of the handbills has come into my possession and is reproduced on page 63. This was an historic match for Norwich City as it was the first match to be played on the "Canaries" new ground at The Nest, Rosary Road, their original pitch being off the Newmarket Road. This milestone of a match was played in pouring rain with the attendance well over 3,000. The result? Norwich City 2, Fulham 1. It is quite possible that with this result No. 24 made a sparkling return trip!

By contrast this enterprising member of the locomotive world on one occasion was given an errand of mercy. During the third week in August 1929 the Leicester express from Norwich was travelling at speed through Guestwick when Samuel Adams the fireman, by some means or other, received severe arm and shoulder injuries when exchanging and picking up the tablet. Driver "Punch" Walpole stopped the train and Melton was alerted. A Midland Railway fireman returning home from his holiday volunteered to fire for Mr Walpole to Melton. On arrival there the injured man was treated by Mr Claud Roper, a leading ambulance man, and immediately transferred into the guard's compartment of a coach waiting and coupled to No. 24 which started at once. With the line cleared by order of Mr (now the late) Percy Youngman right through, Norwich was reached in 26/27 minutes giving an average speed of just over 48mph. This we must remember was over a single track with the tablet to be collected and exchanged at most stations. An eye-witness has related to the author that a goods train was siding shunted at Drayton and No. 24, whistling continuously, raced through the fastest he had ever seen picking up and exchanging the tablet with a loud bang. Fortunately neither staff was dropped. The waiting ambulance at City station soon had fireman Adams in the Norfolk & Norwich Hospital where he recovered after some months, went back to work and was given the light job of firing the South Lynn station pilot cum shunter. It is a pleasure to record at the time of writing, that his two sisters, who ran the Melton tearoom for many years, and his railway brother in Lowestoft, are still with us. Incidentally No. 24 had a different whistle giving an extra low mellow tone.

Coming now to the tenders, these were of the builder's standard design

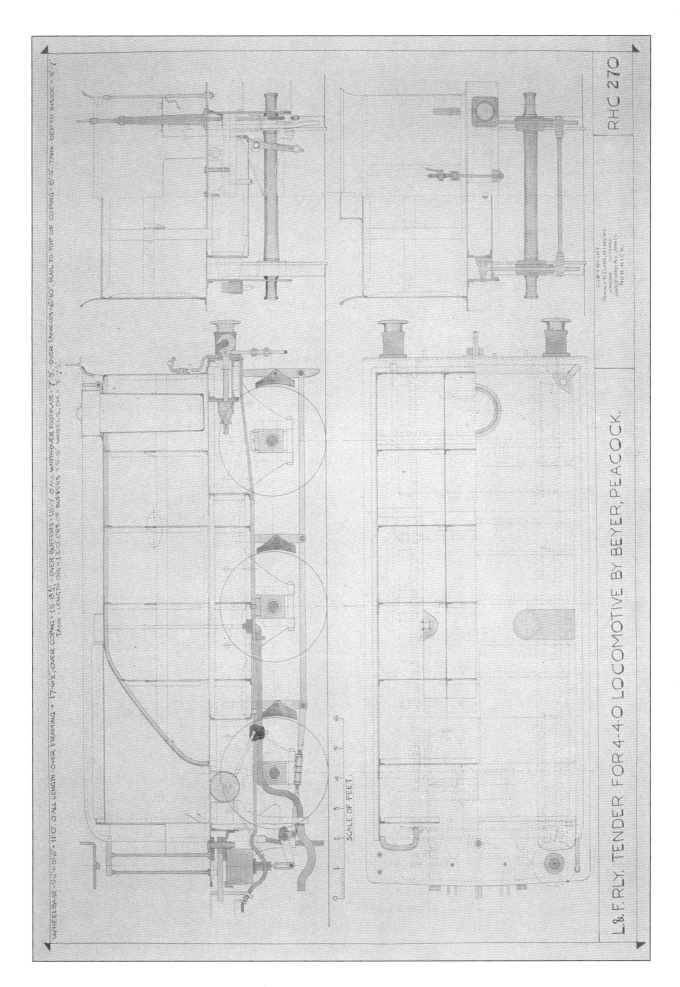

WHEELBASE 5'6" + 5'6" + 11'0" O'ALL LENGTH OVER FRAMING = 17'6'2' OVER COPING = 15'8¼" OVER BUFFERS = 18'-2' O'ALL WIDTH OVER FOOTPLATE 7'5" OVER TANK IOS 6'40' RAIL TO TOP OF COPING B'S TANK DEPTH INSIDE 5'7'. TANK LENGTH IOIS 13'-0' CRES OF BUFFERS 3'5'-8' WHEELS DIA 3'7'2'

SCALE OF FEET

0 1 2 3 4 5 6

L. & F. RLY. TENDER FOR 4-4-0 LOCOMOTIVE BY BEYER, PEACOCK.

RHC 270

and full details can be gleaned from the coloured drawing recorded in *Fig. 13.* Following are the main details:

Wheelbase	5ft 6in + 5ft 6in = 11ft
Length overall over framing	17ft 6½in
Length overall over coping	15ft 8¾in
Length overall over buffers	18ft 9in
Width over footplate	7ft 9in
Width over tanks	6ft 10in
Rail to top of coping	8ft 5in
Tank depth inside	3ft 7in
Tank length outside	13ft
Buffers, centres, horizontally	5ft 8in
Wheels, dia.	3ft 7½in
Water capacity	2,000gall
Coal	3ton
Weight in W.O.	23ton 9cwt
Total weight, engine and tender	61ton 16cwt 1qr

If I have a personal preference it is for the original design rather than for the high straight sided type fitted subsequently.

House magazines and journals issued by the manufacturers provide much of interest about this world-famous firm. It was in May 1854 that Charles F. Beyer and Richard Peacock joined forces to start their works to be known as the Gorton Foundry near Manchester. Previously Mr Beyer, born in Saxony, had been manager for Sharp Brothers and after joining Richard Peacock enlisted a number of German technicians to work in the drawing office. Richard

Plate 34 **Left hand side view of No. 35 awaiting scrapping at Melton in April 1936.**

Peacock had served an apprenticeship with the illustrious Fenton, Murray & Jackson and soon after serving his time became locomotive superintendent of the Leeds & Selby Railway, until 1840 when he joined the GWR. There he worked under Daniel Gooch for a year and then took over the running department of the Manchester, Sheffield & Lincolnshire Railway. So we had one partner fully conversant with management and the other equally qualified in the technical and design side. Their first engine incidentally was completed in July 1855, being one of a batch of eight 2-2-2s for the GWR built for the standard gauge. Like other firms at this period, Beyer, Peacock turned out some highly trained and competent engineers, including Gilbert Claughton and R.H. Burnett who was later the Superintendent of the Metropolitan Railway and who finally returned to Gorton Works, obviously with much experience to offer.

It may not be known generally that additional to the German technicians recruited to the drawing office, Beyer and Peacock from time to time, employed several eminent engineers as consultants.

Perhaps the most famous of these was Mr William Adams who was the third child of John Samuel Adams being born on 15th October 1823 at No. 5 Mill Place, Limehouse. He had served a five years apprenticeship with Messrs Miller & Ravenhill where he became acquainted with many famous engine erectors of the period as his firm was supplying marine engines to the Royal Navy. After experience with Vignoles and the Sardinian Navy he found employment with the Bute West Dock at Cardiff and finally with the North London Railway where, in 1854, he was appointed Locomotive, Carriage and Wagon Superintendent.

Subsequently he evolved his famous 4-4-0 tank engines for the growing suburban traffic utilising his fundamental patent of 13th February 1865, whereby the axles of the bogie wheels could adopt a radial position relative to the curve of the track. At the same time Adams improved the boiler per-

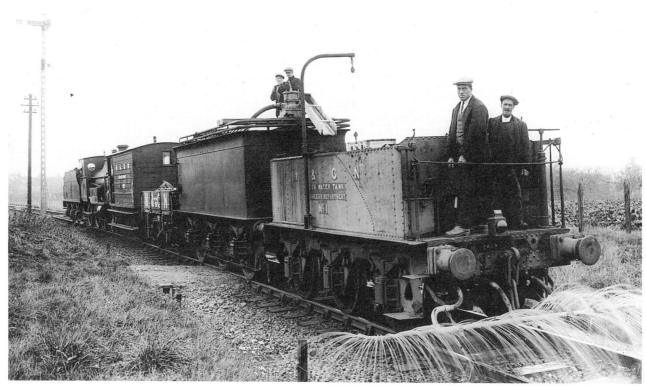

Plate 36 A "Peacock" 4-4-0 on a weed-killing train.

formance and several other items. It was after a period with the GER that Adams became engineer to the London & South Western Railway in 1878.

Small wonder then that the Gorton concern engaged the services of this inventive genius now at Nine Elms. What was particularly noteworthy, from the Lynn & Fakenham aspect, was that Adams' major work at Gorton was to design a fast, light express engine for the Norfolk lines. By now Adams was Chief Engineer of the LSWR, and in 1880 brought out his masterpiece the 135 class 4-4-0 engines with 18in x 24in cylinders using steam at 140psi, and weighing 46 ton 8 cwt.

Wisely, Adams based his Lynn & Fakenham design on his successful 135 class engines. His object all sublime was to incorporate the main details into the Norfolk engines, creating however, a new machine, *not* a scaled down version. By starting from scratch he was able to reduce the dry weight by 8 ton 1 cwt and the cylinder bores were 17in instead of 18in. The grate area he skilfully kept at 17.7 sq ft, as in the London & Southern Western engines.

It was a remarkably clever achievement – the total coming out at 38 ton 7cwt. William Adams' personal record of the Lynn & Fakenham engines was

Plate 37 No. 32 involved in track re-laying at South Lynn.

62

FOOTBALL MATCH AT NORWICH

NORWICH CITY v FULHAM.

Tuesday, 1st Sept., 1908
RETURN TICKETS AT A SINGLE FARE AND A QUARTER

WILL BE ISSUED TO

NORWICH (City Station)

FROM

FAKENHAM, CROMER, MELTON CONSTABLE, DRAYTON

and intermediate stations.

**No less charge than 1/- for an adult passenger.
Fractional parts of a penny are charged as 1d.**

On the forward journey the tickets will only be available by trains due to arrive Norwich after **12.0** noon.

On the return journey the tickets will be available by any train on day of issue only.

Children under three years of age, free; above three and under twelve, half-fares. Tickets are not transferable, and will only be available on the date of issue, and at the stations named; if used on any other day, or at any other stations than those named, the ticket will be forfeited, and the full ordinary charged.

Tickets, Bills and all particulars can be obtained at the stations.

King's Lynn, August, 1908.   JNO. J. PETRIE, Traffic Manager.
350--193/28/8/08.

a photograph of, appropriately, No. 24.

Although reorganised in 1961 for diesel engined locomotives with hydraulic transmission, orders from British Railways failed to appear, owing to the diesel-electric system being preferred. Consequently the great works of 23 acres occupied by Gorton Foundry was dismantled in 1966, and later all shareholders were paid the full face value of their shares.

A few notes on the original painting of this series, Nos 21-24 may prove of interest. In a Beyer, Peacock house journal is to be found the painting specification for these East Anglian engines as follows: "These engines to be painted green with black pointings and white lines, to pattern (from the drawing office apparently). Outside of frames, springs, bogie framing and cylinders to be

painted brown and lined as pattern. Buffers and buffer beams to be vermilion. Engine numbers in gold and shaded with black on both buffer beams. All to be given two finishing coats of Harland & Sons best hard drying body varnish". The remainder of the "Peacocks" were to be painted a chocolate brown lined in black and outlined in chrome yellow. One of the later series had one of the linings in blue as the late Paul Dewhurst informed me. In c1900 the colour was changed to golden gorse (see Chapter XIV), with the frames chocolate and wheels black with matching chrome lining.

I think it most appropriate to conclude this chapter with a typical Beyer, Peacock share certificate which I deem to be a delicately designed work of art.

IX

The Johnsonians – For Passengers

AFTER 1890 the parent companies took more interest in the Joint's motive power than hitherto, so we find our friends Sharp, Stewart using Johnson's Derby drawings to construct 26 most attractive looking 4-4-0, inside cylinder tender passenger engines, resplendent and typical "Johnson" in every way as may be seen from *Plate 38*. They formed part of the MR 2203 class and were built in 1894. The builder's numbers were 3988-4013, and by Melton Constable were numbered 36-39, 42-50, 1-7, 11-14, 17 and 18. In 1896, seven more were ordered, builder's numbers 4190-4196, Melton numbers 51-57.

In *Fig 14* we have a coloured general arrangement drawing of this historic

Plate 38 No. 44, a typical "Johnson" 4-4-0 as supplied to Melton by Sharp, Stewart in 1894.

design from which the main dimensions are listed as follows:

Cylinders	18½ x 26in
Wheels – coupled dia.	6ft 6in
Wheels – bogie dia.	3ft 3in
Wheelbase – bogie	6ft
Wheelbase – bogie to driving	7ft 0½in
Wheelbase – driving	8ft 6in
Wheelbase – total	21ft 6½in
Height to top of chimney	13ft 1$\frac{9}{16}$in
Height to CL of boiler	7ft 4in
Height to top of running plate	4ft 2$\frac{5}{16}$in
Height to CL of buffers	3ft 5in
Overall length of platforms to over buffers	29ft 6in
Overall width	7ft 7in
Buffers – horizontal centres	5ft 8in
Firebox – width inside	3ft 4½
Firebox – length inside	5ft 2$\frac{7}{8}$in
Firebox – maximum height	5ft
Heating surface – firebox	110sq ft
Grate area	17½sq ft
Tubes O/D	244 x 1$\frac{5}{8}$in
Tubes, heating surface	1,130sq ft
Heating surface, total	1,240sq ft
Working pressure	160psi
Boiler, barrel, average dia.	4ft 1in
Boiler, barrel, between tubeplates	10 ft 10$\frac{5}{8}$in
Boiler, shell plates	½in thick
Water capacity	2,950gall
Coal capacity	4ton
Weight in W/O – engine	42ton 17cwt 2qr
Weight in W/O – tender, loaded	33ton 8cwt 3qr
Weight in W/O – total	76ton 6cwt 1qr
Tractive effort @ 80%	13,603lb

Plate 39 **Johnson 4-4-0 No. 54 with Midland type firebox, boiler and short chimney.**

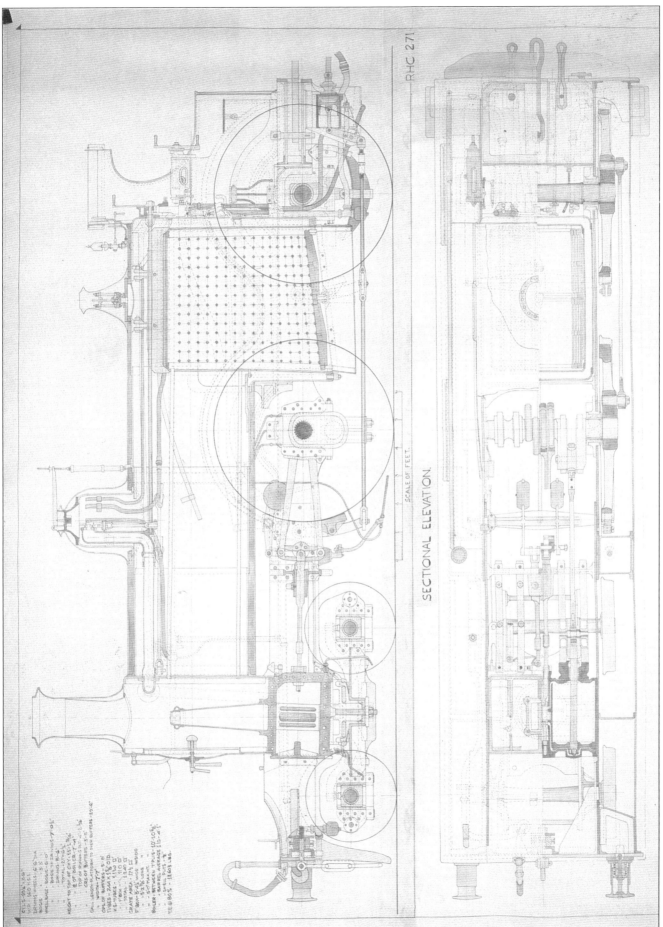

SECTIONAL ELEVATION.

SCALE OF FEET.

RHC 271

Plate 40 No. 44 with a Midland G6 type boiler and new cab.

Plate 41 A classic "Joint" scene as Johnson 4-4-0 No. 37 leaves Hellesdon in 1917 with a Norwich-Melton train.

68

Some minor details are worth mentioning viz, the twin service steam pipes from the dome and parallel to the regulator steam pipe, steam sanding gear for forward running and the graceful curved front platform.

Fig. 15 shows a coloured sectional plan illustrating how the slide valves are neatly placed between the cylinders, link motion with cast iron balance weights and other items probably never previously illustrated.

All with the exception of Nos 48 and 49 and 51-57 were ordered on 5th December 1893. Nos 48 and 49 were ordered early in 1894 and Nos 51-57 on 7th January 1896. No. 1 was delivered on 30th August 1894, Nos 2-18 during August to November 1894, Nos 36-43 on May 1894, Nos 44-47 in June 1894, Nos 48-50 in July 1894, Nos 51-53 in August 1896 and Nos 54-57 during September 1896.

Plate 42 **Construction train at South Lynn headed by No. 5 in April 1900.**

Obviously, owing to its geographical position on the Joint system, all engines were delivered to South Lynn first, and very shortly afterwards allocated to major sheds.

First rebuildings began c1910 and on to 1914. Some were rebuilt more than once, No. 12 for example being rebuilt in 1911, 1924 and 1931.

Several locomotives of this class had one driver for some years continuously. For instance for many years, No. 4 had Tom White and J. Skerry, and it was later to be in the charge of Fred Huggins when stationed at Yarmouth.

These Johnsons were renowned for their performance and on one occasion No. 11 was seen taking 15 bogie coaches up the 1 in 100 out of Saxby to Bourne. Another momentous effort was when No. 54 in the charge of driver Alfred Wallis, and unofficially fired by my friend the late Jack Plummer, got away with 15 bogies out of Sheringham and made a stop at Weybourne. To re-start, Driver Wallis set back until the rear coaches were inclined up the 1 in 100 towards Sheringham and, quickly reversing into full forward gear, got the lot moving by utilising the slack in the couplings. No. 54 at rest is included in *Plate 39.*

Plate 40 shows No. 44 with the Deeley design of chimney fitted to MR type class G6 boiler. The subject of boilers deserves detailed mention. As rebuilding arose the following engines received MR G type boilers:

Locomotive No.	Date of MR Boiler	Class of Boiler
2	1931	G6
6	1930	G6
36	1929	G6
39	1924	G7
44	1930	G6
45	1909	G7
46	1920	G6
	1915	G7
49	1931	G6
50	1929	G6
51	1915	G7
52	1914	G7
53	1910	G7
54	1914	G7
55	1925	G7
56	1913	G7
57	1913	G7
77	1930	G6

Nos 39, 45, 53 and 55 worked Norwich-Leicester on alternate days.

The G7s were fine boilers and easy steamers and had the following main dimensions:

Barrel diameter	4ft 8in
Barrel length front tubeplate to outside throat plate	10ft $5\frac{5}{16}$in
Firebox, length between outside of throat plate and firehole plate	7ft
Crown plate, outside radius	2ft $9\frac{1}{4}$in
Lower front firebox to CL barrel	5ft 6in
Rear bottom of firebox to CL barrel	3ft $10\frac{1}{2}$in
Width maximum outside at top	4ft $11\frac{5}{8}$in
Width maximum inside at top	4ft $0\frac{5}{8}$in
Firebox width outside at bottom	4ft $0\frac{1}{2}$in
Front tubeplate to CL steam dome	7ft 3in
Working pressure	175psi

It must be noted that Nos 39 and 55, during their first rebuilds c1908, were equipped with MR type H boilers set with their centre line eleven inches higher than when new viz 8ft 3in, which in my opinion gave them a more imposing look. Other locomotives of this class not fitted later with G6 or G7 boilers were provided with used boilers "suitable for service" from the stock held at Derby Works, as already noticed in *Plate 40*.

The Joint prided itself on its daily "Leicester Express" starting in three portions from Norwich, Lowestoft and Cromer, the two last portions being united at Melton and taken forward by the Norwich engine, a trip I have enjoyed on many occasions. To ensure reliability four engines, Nos 39, 45, 53 and 55 as noted previously, were kept cosseted and tuned for this special service. They were shedded principally at Norwich City and sped through Norfolk, the Fens and on to Leicester on alternate days.

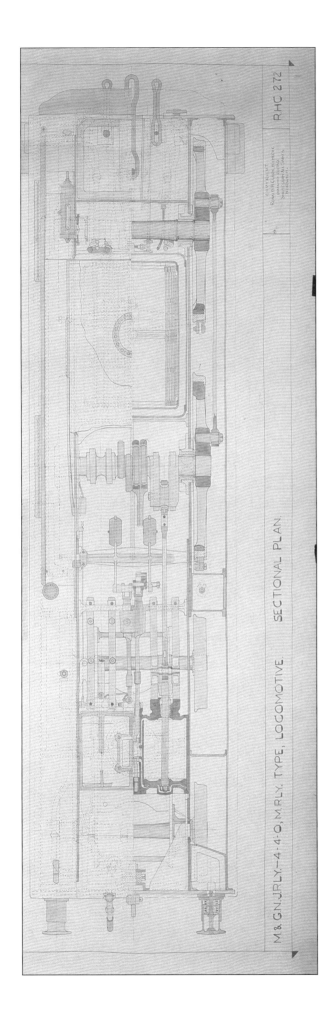

M & GN.JRLY.-4.4.0, M.RLY. TYPE, LOCOMOTIVE.   SECTIONAL PLAN.   RHC 272

Withdrawal dates of this major series of prime movers were as follows:

Locomotive No.	Month	Year
1	November	1937
2	May	1943
3	June	1937
4	February	1938
5	July	1937
6	March	1944
7	June	1937
11	August	1942
12	August	1942
13	September	1941
14	February	1937
17	October	1937
36	–	1937
37	February	1937
38	September	1943
39	February	1937
42	June	1940
43	June	1943
44	August	1941
45	November	1936
46	April	1943
47	April	1942
48	November	1937
49	September	1941
50	January	1945
51	May	1943
52	February	1943
53	January	1940
54	October	1939
55	November	1943
56	November	1953
57	February	1937

Number 47 however suffered a dark and dismal fate being destroyed during a heavy air raid on Norwich during the night of 27th April 1942.

Here I feel it opportune to record a few notes on the firm of Sharp, Stewart & Co. Ltd, often omitted. A Mr Thomas Sharp was joined by a Mr Greenleaves to form Sharp, Greenleaves & Co. in 1811. Thomas's two brothers, Robert Chapman Sharp and John Sharp joined Thomas in 1823 to form Sharp Brothers. They were joined in 1828 by the famous Richard Roberts when it became Sharp, Roberts & Co. Their premises were in Great Bridge Street, Manchester. Thomas Sharp died in 1841 and in 1843 Richard Roberts retired but retained the works, now Atlas Works. This was continued by John Sharp with Thomas Beatt Sharp (son of John) to form Sharp Brothers. John retired in 1852 and his place was taken

Fig. 15 **Sectional plan of the Johnson 4-4-0s.**

Plate 43 **A fine action picture of 4-4-0 No. 56 accelerating 17 bogies from Yarmouth Beach in 1930.**

by Charles Patrick Stewart with the firm now titled Sharp, Stewart & Co. They became a limited liability company in 1864, with Stewart as Chairman until his demise in 1882. The concern now moved from Manchester to Glasgow in 1888 to take over the Clyde Locomotive Works from Neilson.

Some machine tools were produced at first, followed by their first railway locomotive engine called *Experiment* and numbered 32 on the Liverpool & Manchester Railway and constructed in 1833. After becoming Sharp Brothers they built 20 of the famous "Bloomer" class for the LNWR. Additionally to locomotives the firm developed a large trade in foundry work, machine tools and so on. With a full order book the move to Glasgow was a necessity with its larger premises, again known as Atlas Works and which had been established by Walker Montgomerie Neilson in 1884. The first engines built by the Clyde Locomotive Works, it is interesting to note, were eight 4-4-0s for the Highland Railway.

It is not surprising therefore that with Sharp, Stewart now enjoying a world-wide reputation the output from the Atlas Works soon exceeded that from Manchester. It must not be forgotten that the first 4-6-0 locomotives in the United Kingdom and also for the Highland Railway were produced in the old Clyde Works in 1894. They were of course the famous "Jones Goods".

The last change occurred on 12th February 1903 when the three largest locomotive engine builders in Glasgow, Neilson Reid, Sharp, Stewart & Co., and Dübs & Co. amalgamated to form the North British Locomotive Company.

A final historical note worthy of inclusion here. Richard Roberts designed, built and ran a steam carriage in 1833 and the noteworthy feature was his application of the differential to the driving axle, the first example of this bevel wheel train to a road vehicle. The differential as a mechanism and often known as the "Jack in the Box" gear, was first built by Joseph Williamson and incorporated in his bi-facial astronomical clock sometime between the years 1719 and 1725. Williamson was one of the most outstanding clockmakers in London and worked for many years with Samuel Quare. As many readers will know, the differential gear is a most fascinating mechanism to watch in action.

Now to return to East Anglia. There were seven more of this class built by our old friends Beyer, Peacock & Co. Ltd, builder's numbers 4066-4072 and numbered by Melton 74-80. Nos 74-76 were ordered in October 1899 and the remainder in November of that year. Scrapping took place as follows: No. 74 in May 1937, No. 75 in February 1937, No. 76 in July 1943, No. 77 in July 1945, No. 78 in February 1938 and Nos 79 and 80 both in February 1937. As will be noted, No. 77 enjoyed an enviable life of nearly 46 years, only exceeded by No. 50 reaching 51 years. All a great testimony to initial quality

Plate 44 **No. 47 which was to be destroyed in an air raid on Norwich, April 1942.**

and equally to inspired maintenance and skilled driving.

It may be noted here also that the Beyer, Peacock engines, Nos 74-80 were identical to those supplied at the same time to the Midland Railway. Those sent to Derby were there numbered 2581-2590, their 1907 numbers being 473-482.

The variety of tasks these engines performed is well illustrated in *Plate 42* showing No. 5 on a reconstruction train dealing with the alterations to South Lynn station in April 1900. The main buildings had then to be erected.

A good example of how well all Joint engines were maintained is illustrated by the view shown in *Plate 43*. Here we have No. 56 starting 17 bogies out of Yarmouth Beach station in 1930.

A fitting conclusion to this chapter on worthy prime-movers is *Plate 44* which depicts No. 47, the locomotive destroyed by enemy action in Norwich in April 1942.

X

The Three Princes

THE SUCCESS of the famous "Peacocks" proved that 17in x 24in cylinders applied to 6ft driving wheels based on a working pressure of 140psi was a most efficient combination of dimensions for the type of cross-country working abounding on the Joint. Mr Marriott reasoned that any new engines should incorporate these scantlings as the basis of the design, so consequently he obtained sanction from the Joint Committee to design and build three most elegant tank locomotives using similar cylinders, wheels and motion while advantage was taken to increase the working pressure to 160psi. The cylinders, motion and wheels were ordered out from Messrs Beyer, Peacock & Co. Ltd. Melton bestowed upon them the numbers 41, 20 and 9 having been completed

Plate 45 **M&GN 4-4-2T No. 20 in original condition and ready for service.**

in December 1904, February 1909 and March 1910 respectively. No. 41 was withdrawn in January 1944, No. 9 in July 1944 and No. 20 in April 1942. Thus No. 41 had a useful life of 40 years, No. 20 33 years and No. 9 34 years.

No. 41 when completed in December 1904 had the short design of smoke-box but thus was later extended, but numbers 20 and 9 were built with new extended smokeboxes. Later, all were fitted with new Deeley type smokeboxes in the 1920s.

A general arrangement drawing typically coloured of the period is shown in *Fig. 16* and the main dimensions were as follows:

Cylinders	$17\frac{1}{4}$in x 24in
Wheels, coupled dia.	6ft
Later the driving wheels on No. 41 were replaced but whether because of cracks or other faults is not now known.	
Wheels, bogie dia.	3ft
Wheels, trailing dia.	3ft 7in
Wheelbase – bogie	6ft 6in
Wheelbase – bogie centre to driving	10ft 3in
Wheelbase – coupled	8ft 6in
Wheelbase – coupled to trailing	7ft 6in
Wheelbase – total	29ft 6in
Buffer to buffer beam – front	1ft $8\frac{1}{2}$in
Buffer to buffer beam – rear	1ft $8\frac{1}{2}$in
Total	3ft 5in
Buffer beam to CL of front bogie	2ft 3in
Buffer beam to CL of rear trailing axle	3ft 4in
Total	5ft 7in
Total overall length over buffers	38ft 6in
Tubes O/D	240 x $1\frac{5}{8}$in
Heating surface – tubes	1,122sq ft
Heating surface – firebox	110sq ft
Heating surface – total	1,232sq ft (No. 41)
Heating surface – tubes	1,099sq ft (Nos 20 and 9)
Heating surface – total	1,207sq ft (Nos 20 and 9)
Grate area	$17\frac{1}{2}$sq ft
Working pressure	160psi
Firebox length	5ft 4in
Firebox, width	4ft $0\frac{1}{2}$in
Boiler barrel, mean diameter	4ft 2in
Boiler barrel, length between plates	10ft 6in
Rail height to CL of buffers	3ft 5in
Rail height to CL of boiler	7ft 6in
Rail height to top of chimney	12ft $11\frac{9}{16}$in
Tanks, capacity	1,650gall (later 1,600)
Coal capacity	2ton
Tractive effort @ 80%	12,696lb
Adhesive factor	6.26
Weight in W.O.	68ton 9cwt

The boilers were of Deeley design and similar to MR type 36, class B and all fittings followed Derby practice; the closed dome, the Ramsbottom safety valves with the shapely donkey's tail lever, combination injectors mounted on the firebox backhead, and so on. The chimney however was of the Melton third pattern design. These were the only Joint engines to have this particular design of boiler when new and when in for renewals.

The cylinders as ordered out from Beyer, Peacock were bored $17\frac{1}{4}$in. This

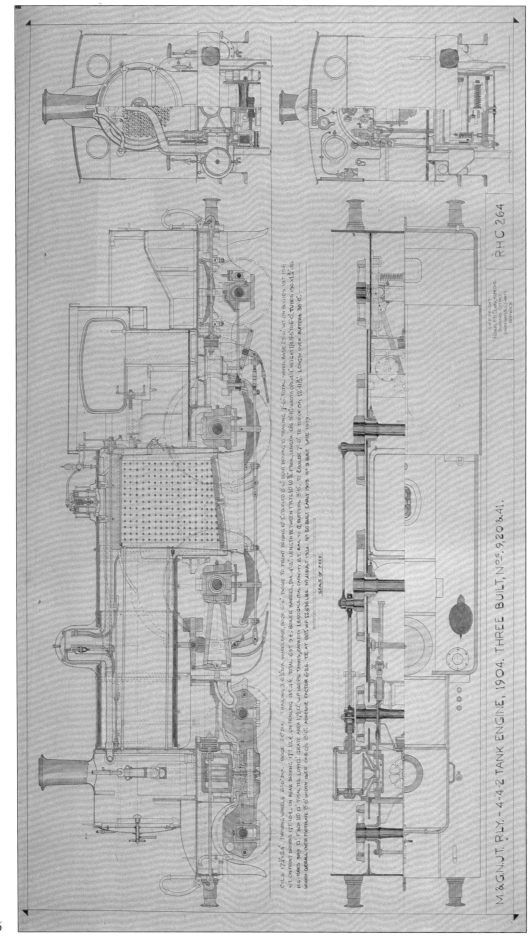

Fig. 16 General arrangement of M&GN 4-4-2Ts.

Plate 46 4-4-2T No. 20 showing the chamfered side tanks to give better forward visibility.

extra piston area gave an increased 1,723lb of loading on the crankpin, thus giving the "Three Princes" a slight advantage over the "Peacocks". Note too the grate area was also increased by 1½sq ft.

Gresham & Holt's steam sanding gear was fitted to work in either direction of running. A view of No. 20 in its original state is to be seen in *Plate 45* ready to depart and outside its local shed. In effect, No. 41 (1904) replaced old No. 41 (*North Walsham*), No. 20 (1909) replaced old No. 20 (*King's Lynn*) and No. 9 (1910) replaced old No. 9 (*Fakenham*). After completion, no entirely new engines were produced at Melton Works.

Although the first of the three, No. 41 left the works in December 1904 it is very interesting to note the final general arrangement drawing bore the typical Melton Drawing Office stencil dated 3rd March 1914 and was initialled "W.M." by William Marriott, the chief, of course.

Later the fronts of the water tanks were cut down or chamfered to provide better vision thus reducing the water capacity by a mere fifty gallons or so. I remember seeing a draughtsman drawing out this modification on one of my several visits to the Melton drawing office and works. *Plate 46* shows No. 20 and illustrates the chamfered side tanks and, which like No. 9, had an extended smokebox.

These delightful machines had certain features rather similar to those on the famous suburban tank engines of the old London, Tilbury & Southend Railway. In those days most Chief Engineers knew each other and met at various Institution meetings, so it is no surprise that Mr Marriott knew Mr Thomas Whitelegg of the LTSR. When asked for details of the trailing frame and axleboxes, Mr Whitelegg loaned a tracing to the Chief at Melton.

In *Plate 47* we have a view depicting No. 41 during its erection at Melton and towards the end of 1904. Note particularly the very neat fitting of the wooden strips forming the cylinder lagging to be covered ultimately by the planished sheet steel. Painting of these engines, although it might not have been identical for other types, comprised one coat for filling and rubbing down, two of primer of pure genuine English Stack white lead; followed by two of the main coat, all rubbed down and then finished by one of Harland & Sons No. 2001 Hard Drying Body Varnish also rubbed down and lastly, the final coat of varnish. Very princely they looked when finished.

This royal trio was used principally on the Norfolk & Suffolk Joint lines and they were shedded usually at Cromer, Yarmouth and one, in some summer months, at Lowestoft. For sometime No. 9 was stationed at South Lynn and often did I see it taking the afternoon train to Spalding. Upon Grouping all had the usual "0" prefix to their numbers.

The author's last memories of one of the Princes, No. 9, was in a siding at Thursford station with the front end lifted by sheerlegs to repair a front bogie axlebox which obviously had run very hot.

Another illustration is included in *Plate 48* which is a 3½in gauge model of one of the 4-4-2 tanks, No. 9 acquired by my late father shortly after the

Plate 47 The first 4-4-2T, No. 41 during erection in Melton shops in late 1904.

Plate 48 The author's 3½in gauge model of 4-4-2T No. 9.

prototype was completed. Unfortunately the maker and exact date are unknown. An important point is that it is painted to match accurately the Melton coloured master board once shown at a M.&G.N. Circle meeting. The golden gorse of the model may therefore be taken as correct. As one cannot scale nature the model has several fittings, burner fuel pump and so on, not of course applicable to No. 9 in full size.

A little story can now be told about the present framed and glazed village sign at each main road approach to Melton Constable. The then local council, uninformed as these organisations always are, had proposed one of the Manchester-built engines to be used on the sign! I was quick to note the proposal published in the local press and submitted a terse letter to the editor pointing out how extraordinary and incongruous it was that a locomotive made in the local works had not been proposed, especially as sufficient details existed to enable any competent signwriter to make a correct and attractive outline. Within a few days a pair of officials visited me and departed with the information required. The result is the authentic picture now seen by the side of the B1354 road and is to be enjoyed in *Plate 49.*

If only one of these elegant machines had been preserved . . .

XI

The Johnsonians – For Goods

NOT ONLY was the passenger haulage aspect dealt with by the parent companies but attention was concentrated simultaneously on extra motive power for heavy goods working over the grades, arduous for such working, and abundant east of Lynn Regis.

Again the Midland Railway tackled the situation by permitting S.W. Johnson to lend drawings of his 0-6-0 tender goods engines Class D (2284), to two builders viz Messrs Neilson & Co. and Kitson & Co. Eight locomotive engines were ordered from each firm. Let us study with quiet calm deliberation the Neilson machines first.

These bore Neilson builder's numbers 5032 to 5039 and had the following detailed dimensions:

Cylinders	18in x 26in
Wheels dia.	5ft 2$\frac{1}{2}$in
Wheelbase	8ft + 8ft 6in
Wheelbase, total	16ft 6in
Height to top of chimney	12ft 11$\frac{1}{2}$in
Height to underside of cab roof	11ft 0$\frac{3}{16}$ in
Height to CL of boiler	7ft 1 $\frac{15}{16}$ in
Height to top of running plate	4ft 2 $\frac{13}{16}$ in
Boiler dia. of barrel outside	4ft 1in
Boiler length between tubeplates	10ft 10in
Boiler tubes O/D	244 x 1$\frac{5}{8}$in
Firebox length	5ft 2$\frac{7}{8}$in
Firebox width	3ft 4$\frac{1}{2}$in
Firebox depth at front	6ft
Heating surface – tubes	1,130sq ft
Heating surface – firebox	110sq ft
Heating surface – total	1,240sq ft
Grate area	17$\frac{1}{2}$sq ft
Working pressure	150psi
Buffers, horizontal centres	5ft 8in
Length overall	27ft 9$\frac{9}{16}$ in
Weight in W.O.	38ton 16cwt
Tractive effort @ 80% W.P.	16,078lb

Further details of both dimensions and the picturesque outline are illustrated very clearly in the coloured general arrangement drawing included in *Fig. 17* showing also a sectional plan. Note the very stout and substantial weighshaft and the nest of four eccentrics ingeniously tucked in between the massive cranks.

Plate 50 shows No. 59 in its original form when new from the builders, the batch being fitted with both steam and vacuum brake gear. Thus fitted and with their 5ft 2½in driving wheels they were soon found to be very useful on passenger work, including through excursion trains in the various seasons as I can readily testify. Finding goods engine appropriate also for passenger work was not peculiar to East Anglia as the famous "Jones Goods" of the Highland Railway were also detailed for such work.

When first received at Melton Mr Marriott allotted them the numbers 58-65. The inevitable boiler replacements occurred in due course and so we find No. 62 sported two boilers during its lifetime, ie a MR class H in 1906 followed by a class G7 made in 1923 but drawn from the Derby boiler bank and fitted in 1924. After closure of Melton Shops in 1936 No. 62 went to Stratford Works where in March 1937 it had various extra plates added for strengthening. The replacement boilers incidentally were pressed now to 160psi. G7 boilers necessitated the centre line being raised to 7ft 7 $\frac{7}{8}$ in above rail level. At the same time the driving wheels were re-tyred and finished at 5ft 3in diameter.

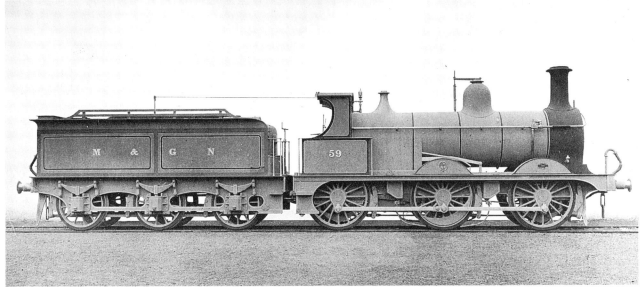

Their tenders had wheels 4ft 2½in diameter, horizontal centres of buffers 5ft 8in, a water capacity of 2,950 gallons, space for four tons of coal and in working order weighed 33ton 10cwt 3qr. Total weight of engine and tender 72ton 6cwt 3qr. Other modifications during re-building included the Deeley design of smokeboxes and Melton pattern chimneys.

Withdrawal dates were as follows: No. 58 in 1938, No. 62 in 1939, No. 60 in 1941, No. 61 in 1942, Nos 59, 63 and 64 in 1944 and finally No. 65 in 1947. To work for over forty years, grappling with chalky Norfolk water was certainly no mean feat.

The firm of Neilson & Co. was first established by Walter Neilson and James Mitchell as Neilson & Mitchell in premises in McAlpine Street, Glasgow in either 1836 or 1837. They commenced making stationary and marine engines of various types. Soon a Mr Kerr joined them so that towards the end of 1837 their title had become Kerr, Mitchell & Neilson and had transferred to new property in Hyde Park Street. Titles changed quickly at this period and by 1840 they styled themselves Kerr, Neilson & Co. However Mr Kerr departed, so in 1845 their establishment was known as Neilson & Mitchell. Their first locomotives appeared in 1843 when three 0-4-0s were built for the Glasgow, Garnkirk & Coatbridge Railway on a 4ft 6in gauge. A most famous stationary engine designed and constructed by Neilson & Mitchell in 1842 was the rope-haulage engine for the Cowlairs Incline. In 1845 the firm became plain

Plate 50 **Midland Railway type 0-6-0 goods locomotive No. 59, from the builder's official photograph.**

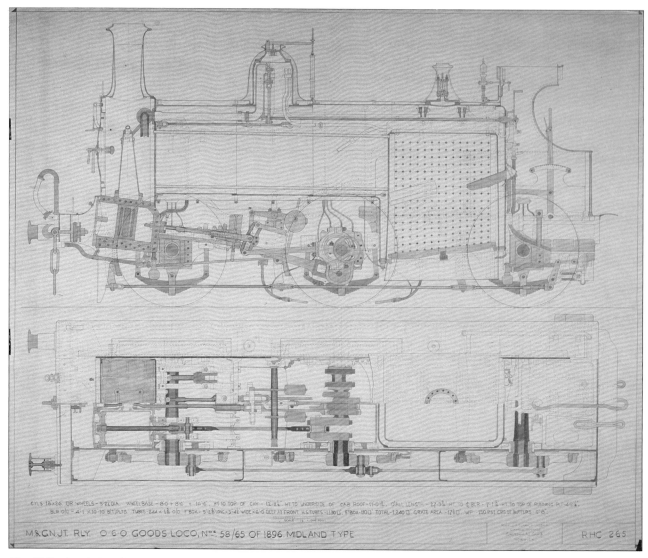

CYLS 18×26. DR WHEELS- 5′2″DIA. WHEELBASE - 8-0 + 8-6 = 16-6″. HT TO TOP OF CHY - 12-11½″. HT TO UNDERSIDE OF CAB ROOF-11-0½″. O'ALL LENGTH - 27-5¼″ HT TO ⊄ BLR - 7-1½″ HT TO TOP OF RUNNING PLT-4'2¾″.
BLR O/D - 4-1″ X 10-10 BT'PLTS. TUBES- 2.44 × 1⅝ O/D. F'BOX - 5'2⅞"LONG × 3-4½" WIDE × 6-0 DEEP AT FRONT. H.S TUBES - 1130 ☐. F'BOX-110 ☐. TOTAL- 1,240 ☐. GRATE AREA - 17⅔ ☐. WP- 150 PSI. CRS OF BUFFERS - 5-8″.

M & G N. JT. RLY.   0-6-0 GOODS LOCO, Nᵒˢ. 58/65 OF 1896. MIDLAND TYPE   RHC 265

Fig. 17 **Sectional elevation and plan of the Johnson 0-6-0 goods engines for the M&GN.**

Neilson & Co, but in 1888 Walter Neilson severed his connection with the concern when their title once again enjoyed a change to Neilson, Reid & Co. with James Reid the only proprietor. Thus it remained until 1903 when, as we have seen, it combined with Dübs & Co. and Sharp, Stewart & Co., to form the North British Locomotive Company.

It is curious how certain firms seem to attract outstanding and competent men. For example, Benjamin Connor became works manager to Walter Neilson. Then Henry Dübs, Patrick Stirling and James Reid all fulfilled important posts with Neilson for a time and a good grounding they obviously absorbed as proved by their later achievements. Henry Dübs later commenced on his own in 1864 in Polmadie and called his premises Queen's Park Works.

When Walter Neilson left in 1884 he set up on his own in Springburn calling his works the Clyde Locomotive Works which as we have noted, built the famous 4-6-0s for the Highland Railway after which, in 1888 it was purchased by Sharp, Stewart & Co.

Again let us return to East Anglia, when yet another famous builder has to be considered viz Kitson & Co, Ltd of the Airedale Foundry, Jack Lane, Leeds. They supplied eight more identical Johnson Goods, their work's numbers being 3873-3880 and numbered at Melton 66-73. They were all delivered in 1899. No. 60 and 71 both acquired G7 boilers in 1921. Rebuilding dates were No. 66 in 1921, No. 67 in 1917, Nos 68-71 in 1921, No. 70 in 1923, No. 72 in 1920 and No. 73 in 1918. No. 69 had had a previous rebuild in 1908. Like the rest of their class they had a long and useful life. Nos 66, 67, 68 and 72 were withdrawn 1937, No. 73 in 1941, No. 69 in 1942, No. 71 in 1943 and No. 70 in 1944. No. 70 closely emulating No. 77 but not reaching the record of No. 50.

I have seen statements that some of these Johnsonian Goods had cylinders greater than 18in bore. This was the size when new but after two or more "trueings up", the final dimension could be $18\frac{1}{4}$in or even $18\frac{1}{2}$in as Mr A.H. Nash once pointed out to me.

Here again I think it appropriate to record some brief notes on Kitsons. It was one James Kitson who started up his Airedale Foundry in Leeds in 1835 quickly taking into partnership one Charles Todd. They were joined in 1838 by David Laird, a wealthy farmer but he left them in 1842. Charles Todd also left at this period as did James Shepherd and this duumvirate set up in opposition to Kitson. Up to 1838 the firm was plain James Kitson but from this date it was Todd, Kitson & Laird and within the year it changed once again to Kitson & Laird. Sometimes the names were confused and it has been recorded at this time as Laird & Kitson! However Kitson was joined by Isaac Thompson and William Hewitson to form Kitson, Thompson & Hewitson.

The year 1858 saw Thompson depart but Hewitson kept on with Kitson until his (Hewitson's) death in 1863. It was now more generally known as Kitson & Hewitson but c1863 it adopted its final title of Kitson & Co. It is most interesting to record that Charles Todd had served his apprenticeship with the famous Matthew Murray at the Round Foundry in Holbeck. Murray is well known for many great achievements not the least being his invention in 1801 of his hypocycloidal straight line motion – a delightful mechanism to watch in motion. Kitson's first locomotive was *Lion* in 1838, an 0-4-2 with 5ft coupled wheels. Sadly for Kitsons, in later years orders fell off and a receiver was appointed in 1934, the last locomotive being built for the Jamaican Government in 1938.

In later years the soul of the firm was the late Lt Col. E. Kitson Clark. Not only was he a fine engineer but also a classics scholar. It was he who composed the motto of The Newcomen Society for the study of the history of engineering and technology: *Actorem memores simul affectamus agenda* (whilst looking to the future never neglect the lessons of the past).

A charming story will form a fitting conclusion to this chapter. Lt. Col. Kitson Clark wrote an immortal classic *Kitsons of Leeds,* being his history of his family firm 1837-1937 and published as a centenary volume. It is known probably to many readers. A lady once asked the Colonel if he would kindly parse the title. "Certainly", came the instant reply, "Kitsons is in Leeds and are engineers".

XII

The Ivatt Contribution

EVEN WITH the 16 elegant Johnson goods engines Melton was often hard pressed to find sufficient locomotive power for its increasing goods, special excursions and sometimes for the Lowestoft and Yarmouth fish traffic, and asked Mr H.A. Ivatt of The Plant at Doncaster if he could help out. At this period, 1899-1900, the GNR had on order from Dübs & Co., 36 0-6-0 tender goods locomotives of their Class J4 type. One dozen of this order was diverted to Melton in 1901 bearing Dübs works numbers 3933-3944. Mr Marriott numbered them 81-92 and classed them DA, with No. 90 being illustrated in *Plate 51*.

A coloured general arrangement drawing comprising five fully detailed

Plate 51 **Ivatt designed 0-6-0, M&GN Class DA No. 90.**

views is shown in *Fig. 18* and from which the following scantlings have been prepared:

Cylinders	$17\frac{1}{2}$in x 26in
Cylinders, inclination	1ft $8\frac{3}{4}$in
Cylinders, horizontal CL	2ft $4\frac{1}{2}$in
Cylinders, slide valve travel	$6\frac{1}{2}$in
Cylinders, angle A of advance	90° + 18° = 108°R.H.
Cylinders, angle B of advance	90° - 17° = 107° L.H.
Cylinders, valve lap	$1\frac{1}{8}$in R.H. Crank leads
Driving wheel dia.	5ft $1\frac{1}{2}$in
Boiler – barrel O/D	4ft $9\frac{1}{4}$in
Boiler – length between tubeplates	10ft $4\frac{1}{8}$in
Boiler – tubes	213 x $1\frac{3}{4}$in O/D x 10ft $2\frac{1}{2}$in long
Firebox, length	4ft $9\frac{3}{4}$in
Firebox, width	3ft $4\frac{1}{4}$in
Firebox, height	5ft $10\frac{9}{16}$ in
Firebox, grate area	$16\frac{1}{4}$sq ft
Heating surface, tubes	1,016sq ft
Heating surface, firebox	103sq ft
Heating surface, total	1,119sq ft
Working pressure	175psi
Height overall to top of chimney	13ft $1\frac{1}{16}$ in
Height rail to centre line of boiler	7ft $3\frac{1}{2}$in
Wheelbase, leading to driving	7ft 3in
Wheelbase, centre to trailing	8ft 3in
Wheelbase, total	15ft 6in
Weight in W.O. leading axle	14ton 3cwt 2qr
Weight in W.O. driving axle	14ton 14cwt
Weight in W.O. trailing axle	12ton 5cwt
Weight in W.O. total	41ton 2cwt 2qr
Length overall	26ft $8\frac{1}{8}$ in
Width overall	8ft
Tractive effort @ 80%	18,126lb

Plate 52 illustrates No. 83 in its original condition.

An indication of the great attention paid to every detail in the design is illustrated by the one degree of difference between the angles of advance of the eccentrics, viz 108° for the right hand crank and 107° for the left hand. Note too the firebox crown sheet and outer casing plate are tied together by 110 tie-bolts, very similar to the method used by Charles Burrell & Sons in their road locomotive boilers, being of course smaller where only 32 ties were used. The whistle mountings are inside the cab. Another interesting detail was that both engine and tender were fitted with vacuum brake gear. All were delivered in October 1901 and later rebuilding dates were as follows:

No. 81 June and No. 86 October 1927, No. 87 in May 1925 and again in June 1937. In 1926 No. 85 in April, No. 89 and 90 in February, with No. 91 in the January. No. 85 again rebuilt in February 1937, No. 89 again in April that year and No. 91 again in May 1937. December 1924 saw a rebuild of No. 84 and again in January 1937. Nos 82, 83 and 92 in August, January and October respectively in 1921 and lastly, No. 88 in November 1920. During rebuilding the new and larger boilers had barrels 4ft 8in diameter.

It should be pointed out that most of this series, like all the others, under went minor alterations, modifications and additions etc. Nearly all had Mr A.H. Nash's design of chimney (seen in *Plate 53*) fitted, which were removed at Stratford Works in 1937. No. 85 for example had a GNR C12 chimney and

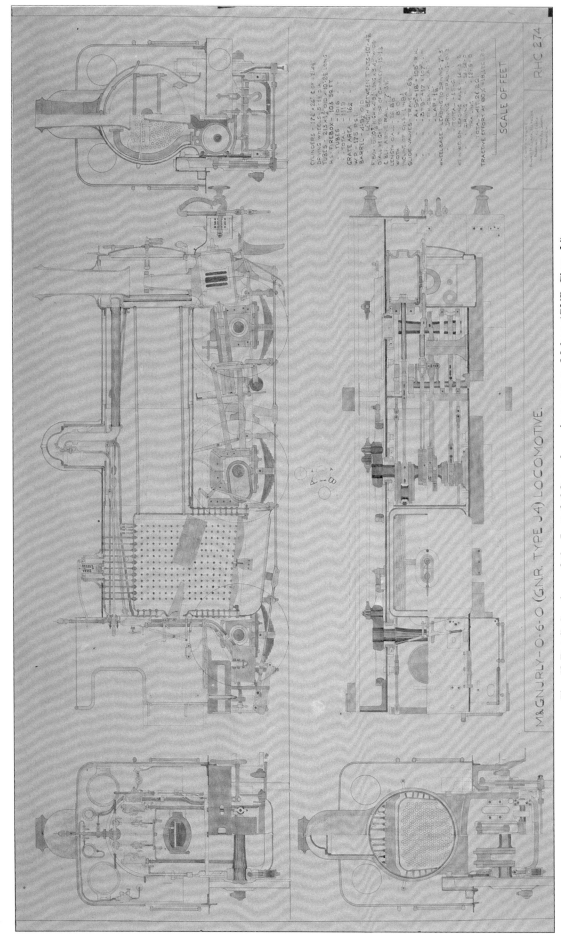

CYLINDERS - 17½"×26" 6 OF 2-¼"
DRIVING WHEELS-5'-1½" DIA
TUBES - 215"×4" O/D AND 10'-2¾" long
H.S. FIREBOX - 103 SQ.FT
TUBES - 1018
TOTAL - 1162
GRATE AREA - 16.2
W.P.-175 %L
BARREL - 4'-9½" O/D

FROM 6-07 HIGH ×3'-4½ WIDE ×5'-4 HIGH
CHALLENGE RANGE OF O.D.INSIDE 2.3/4"
C & H.J.SHELL CLAD 36. 8'-7¾"
LENGTH IN - 8. 0 5
WIDTH IN - 1. 8 0
INCLINE OF CUT - 1 N 18.1
SLIDE VALVES - TRAVE - 6½"
                      - A.90"+18".106" R H.
                      - B.90".41" 1.17" L H.
                      - LAP.5/4"
WHEELBASE - LEADING TO DRIVING-7-3
              - DRIVING TO TRAILING-8-3
              - TOTAL - 15-6
WT. IMPO. ON LEADING AXLE 14. 10. 0
              - DRIVING 14. 18. 0
              - TRAILING 15. 2. 0
              - TOTAL 44. 10. 0
TRACTIVE EFFORT AT 80% = 18946 LB

SCALE OF FEET

M&GN.JRLY-0-6-0 (GNR. TYPE J4) LOCOMOTIVE.

RHC 274

Fig. 18 Detail drawings of the Ivatt 0-6-0 goods engines sent to Melton (GNR Class J4).

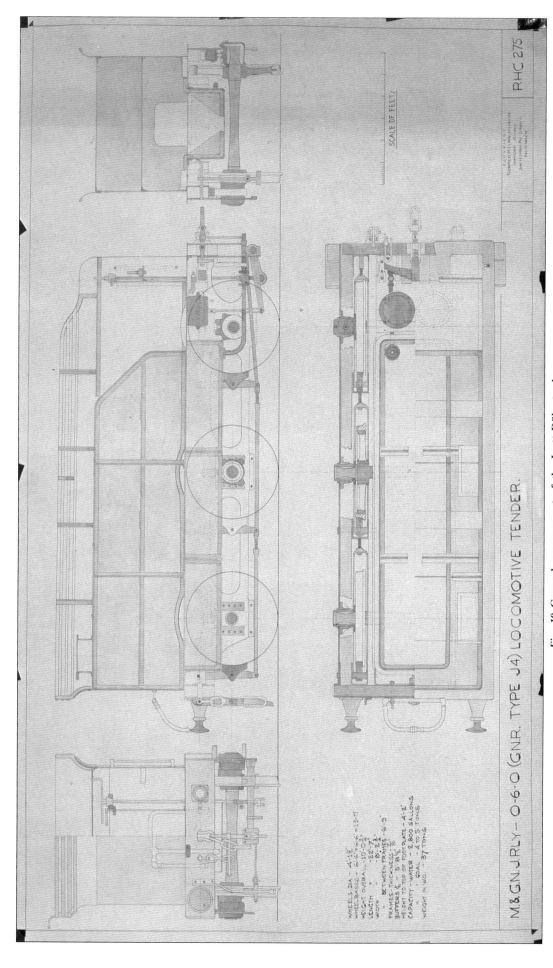

M.&G.N.J.RLY.- 0·6·0 (G.N.R. TYPE J4) LOCOMOTIVE TENDER.

SCALE OF FEET.

WHEELS DIA. - 4'·1½"
WHEEL BASE - 6'·6"+6'·6" = 13'·0"
HEIGHT OVERALL - 10'·0½"
LENGTH " - 22'·7¼"
WIDTH " - 8'·2¼"
     BETWEEN FRAMES - 6'·5"
FRAMES THICKNESS - 1"
BUFFERS C.L. - 5'·8½"
HEIGHT TO TOP OF FOOT PLATE - 4'·2"
CAPACITY WATER - 2,800 GALLONS
     "   COAL - 4 TO 5 TONS
WEIGHT IN W.O. - 37 TONS

Fig. 19 General arrangement of the Ivatt-Dübs tenders.

No. 86 had one of a stovepipe design. Then too, all had their smokeboxes extended in 1907 and brass numerals fixed at various dates in the 1920s. Nos 83 and 88 in 1920; Nos 82 and 92 in 1921; No. 84 in 1924; No. 87 in 1925; Nos 85, 89 and 90 in 1926; Nos 81, 86 and 91 in 1927.

If one studies the general arrangement drawings of both the Johnson and Ivatt designs their similarity is readily apparent. For example there is only one inch difference in driving wheel diameters, half an inch in cylinder bores, a common stroke of 26in and so on. One cannot help wondering, possibly a little mischievously, if one designer studied the other's drawings! But to be fair, most designs were illustrated in the technical press of the period.

Coming now to the tenders, we find they had the following main dimensions:

Wheel, dia.	4ft 1½in
Wheelbase	6ft 6in +
	6ft 6in = 13ft
Height overall	10ft 0¾in
Length overall	22ft 7in
Width overall	8ft 2¾in
Width between frames	6ft 9in
Frames, thickness of plates	⅞in
Buffers. Horizontal centre lines	5ft 8½in
Height to top of footplate	4ft 2in
Capacity, water	2,800gall
Capacity, coal	4 to 5ton
Weight in W.O.	37ton

Comparison with the Beyer, Peacock tenders shows the GNR design had fewer anti-surge plates, coal rails additional and no long intake duct. All the main details are shown clearly in the four views in the coloured drawings in *Fig. 19*.

Although the GNR's own drawings refer to these engines as their "J4 Type", later in LNER days they became "Class J3". After the change in administration at Melton in 1936, they all received the prefix "0" and as such, Nos 082, 084, 085, 087 and 089-092 were fitted with boilers with a barrel diameter of 4ft 5in. These locomotives were then reclassified back to their original Class J4. An odd man out was No. 081 which acquired another boiler with a diameter of 4ft 8in.

Another re-numbering took place in 1946 when the LNER bestowed upon some the numbers 4156-4167. In the record books BR later prefixed a "6" to numbers 4158, 4160, 4162, 4163 and 4167, but as far as I can discover only No. 4160 ever ran as 64160. Being by this time pretty well worn and aged, BR took them out of service so that Nos 90 and 91 went in 1946, Nos 81, 82, 84, 86 and 89 in 1947, No. 92 in 1948, No. 88 in 1949, No. 87 in 1950 and lastly, Nos 83 and 85 in 1951. Strangely, although No. 86 was withdrawn in June 1939, it was returned to active service in the following October. A view of one of the rebuilds, No. 62 is included in *Plate 54*.

Here I think it opportune to refer to the locomotive situation on the Joint

Plate 52 Works' photograph of 0-6-0 No. 83, Dübs 3935 of 1901.

in the period a few years before, and a shorter period after, its formation in 1893. On the E&MR lines west of Lynn, Midland 2-4-0s, aided by a few ancient 2-2-2s worked most of the traffic. The Great Northern also helped out with the loan of some 0-4-2 tender engines and all operated on the Bourne, Spalding and Lynn services. Two favourites were Nos 556 and 557 and a view of the latter forms *Fig. 28* in my *Scenes on the M&GN* (Moorland, 1978). After E&MR days and the arrival of the Johnsons and Ivatts for the Joint, these borrowed engines returned to their homelands. Even in early Joint days one or two Midland, Kirtley 2-4-0 tender engines were to be found, mainly on the Cromer branch. However in most cases they had been overhauled at Melton and when being run-in were made to earn their keep for a week or so, working in revenue-earning service! As these were never owned by the Joint they scarcely come within the scope of this book.

A final historical note to this chapter. When, as we have previously noticed, Henry Dübs the managing partner, severed his association with Walter Neilson in 1863, he commenced on his own account the next year, building

his own locomotive manufactory in Little Govan, later named just Govan. The site he chose was fortuitously excellent clay and the excavated material was used to make the necessary bricks on the spot. His first locomotive, completed in 1865, was part of an order from the Caledonian Railway for ten 0-4-2s with driving wheels 5ft 2in diameter and cylinders 16½in x 22in. When he left Neilson he apparently enticed Neilson's chief draughtsman, Samson George Goodall-Copestake, to accompany him and work in the same capacity. As I have recorded previously, Henry Dübs joined with Sharp, Stewart and Neilson, Reid to form the North British Locomotive Company in 1903 and retaining the familiar diamond-shaped builder's plate.

Plate 53 Ivatt 0-6-0 No. 68 showing A.H. Nash's design of stovepipe chimney and G7 type boiler. Photographed at Melton Constable in 1938.

Plate 54 DA class 0-6-0 No. 62 in its final rebuilt, Melton form.

XIII

The Saloon of the Engineers

AS WE HAVE noticed in *Plate 12,* Chapter IV, this unusual Engineer's Inspection Saloon was often hauled by one of the Seven Sisters, in that instance No. 20 it is believed. Although there exist several photographs of this carriage, few other details are available of this "one off" vehicle. Fortunately however I have been able to prepare the drawing reproduced in *Fig. 20* which provides also, details and general arrangements of its layout. Axle springing was taken care of by multi-leafed semi-elliptical springs, as were the drawbars, giving a smooth and shockless start. Continuous brake gear was fitted to the end pairs of wheels and there was also a hand brake operated by the wheel shown in both elevation and plan. Note also the comfortable couch with ornamental legs, a private privy and the external ladder giving access to the "coachman's" seat for inspecting the inside of arches and the Toft Tunnel.

The main dimensions of this interesting passenger vehicle were as follows:

Length over buffers	35ft 2in
Length over buffers corner pillars	31ft 6in
Length over headstocks	31ft 5in
Width over bulks	9ft 2in
Width over step boards	8ft 6in
Width inside	7ft 4in
Rail to ventilator top	11ft 11½in
Rail to floor level	4ft 3in
Rail to centreline of buffers	3ft 5in
Wheels, dia.	3ft 6½in
Wheelbase	20ft
Centres of journals	6ft 7½in
Drawing completed	5th June 1902
Company's number allotted	2

Further details can be seen in *Plate 55* showing an excellent external view of No. 2 which complements the details in the two previous illustrations.

Every so often East Anglia received unseasonal rainfalls, and a year noted and remembered for a severe and sustained cloudburst, was 1912. On 26th August that year a gross rainfall of no less than 7½in occurred over an area of 1,039 square miles. In total about one third of the annual average rainfall fell in twelve hours! Many slips and washouts resulted including a small bridge near Hellesdon where the embankment was partially destroyed. Immediate repair work needed surveillance and inspection. The scene is vividly recorded in *Plate 56* showing the ever-reliable No. 9A with the saloon at the site of the disaster and the accompanying activity.

A daughter of Mr Marriott told me that always on his birthday, besides the officials, the whole family took possession of No. 2, and father always found it necessary to carry out inspections during the summer months on the lines to Cromer, Sheringham, Mundesley or Yarmouth. So a happy day at the seaside was enjoyed by all! These little incidents help to illustrate the matey and happy type of organisation the "Joint" really was.

Plate 55 **The Engineer's Saloon attached to 4-4-0T No. 20, with the "Inspectorate" alongside.**

Plate 56 **Following the 1912 floods, 4-4-0T No. 9A heads the Inspection Saloon at Hellesdon.**

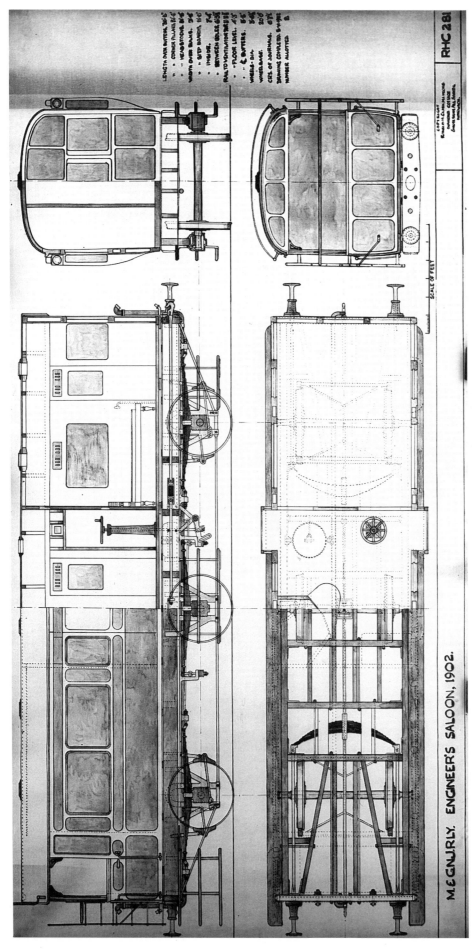

Fig. 20 General arrangement of the Engineer's Saloon.

92

XIV

Filling the Gaps

IT IS ALMOST impossible to weave some facts and lore into the pattern of mechanical and engineering details covered thus far, therefore a separate chapter becomes, in my opinion, something of a necessity. It also enables the author to include some items so far omitted.

The famous Melton Works has been mentioned so far in every chapter. What was it like? An inkling may already have been gained or suggested by one of the Three Princes in *Plate 47*. Let us commence with the famous erecting or fitting shop of which a view from the overhead travelling crane at the east end is to be seen in *Plate 57*, where eight engines are being dealt with. The first, on the extreme left was in for regulator adjustments and other minor items. The other view, in *Plate 58* shows four locomotives nearing completion with a Peacock, probably No. 31, on the first left. These illustrations should be studied conjointly. This large shop was 210ft x 60ft.

The lighter machine shop, 120ft x 40ft, is shown in *Plate 59* where the smaller parts were produced and also where one cannot fail to notice the multiplicity of belts. Heavy wheel and axle turning was done in an adjacent bay detailed in *Plate 60*. Driving wheels were accommodated in the large lathe to

Plate 57 Melton Constable Works erecting shop, viewed from the overhead travelling crane.

Plate 58 **Another view of the erecting shop.**

Plate 59 **The light machine shop at Melton.**

the right in the picture and could turn wheels up to 7ft in diameter. Both these pictures are full of appeal. Power was provided by a large horizontal steam engine.

During World War I Melton Works, like many other similar centres, turned out large quantities of war material and in *Plate 61* we have a bar cutting machine cutting off blanks for 18 pounder shells. Alongside will be seen roughly forged connecting rods awaiting machining. Note the Kitson 0-6-0 No. 69 on the right, background.

Many non-perishable items were of necessity stored outside and a miscellaneous but valuable collection of wheels, axles, chimneys and steam domes is shown in *Plate 62*. Note the hand-operated pillar jib crane by the end wall. This and other yards were served by the works' own 2ft gauge track operated

Plate 60 Melton's heavy machine shop.

Plate 61 The bar-cutting machine at Melton, cutting blanks for 18lb shells during World War I.

by flat-topped trucks, hand-propelled with the tracks having turntables at their ends and other strategic points well illustrated in *Plate 63*. Here I may mention that during World War I many lengths of 2ft gauge Decauville type track, points and turnouts were fabricated in this yard and forwarded for use in Flanders.

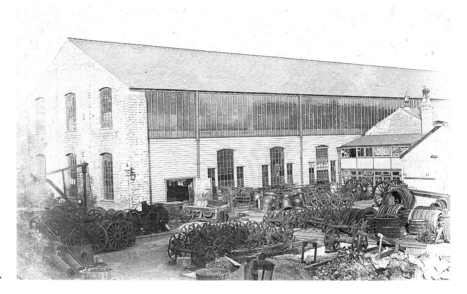

Plate 62 **The spares yard at Melton Works.**

The largest shop near the south boundary was the boiler shop, 130ft x 35ft. Also other yards had standard gauge tracks exemplified in *Plate 64* which served the south side and was also used to park locomotives awaiting attention for some minor fault or other. This photograph was taken in the early days of the works and shortly after it was brought into operation.

In the first few years after opening some heavy lifting for wheel removal was carried out in the south yard using the sheerlegs seen clearly in *Plate 65*. A close examination of the original print shows the object under lift is a tender off one of the Cornish Derivatives. In the right hand background is a tender off a Peacock and in front a two-plank sided wagon. The tenders are lettered *M.&.G.N.* but the wagon *Jt.M.&.G.N.*

The large engine shed juxta the turntable was 130ft x 45ft and across the sidings was the foundry, 90ft x 30ft and joining it end on was, of all departments, the mess room! This latter however was only 80ft long.

Next came the main running sheds. *Plate 66* is a grand view of the three-road large shed. From left to right the partially visible engine is No. 34, left

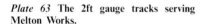

Plate 63 **The 2ft gauge tracks serving Melton Works.**

Plate 64 The South Yard, Melton.

Plate 65 The large sheerlegs in South Yard, Melton.

in the shed is No. 31, middle No. 12, right hand end, No. 26 and the tender just visible outside right is of No. 32. Yet another view of South Lynn Shed and yard, taken about the same time, is to be seen in *Plate 67* and shows a front view of No. 59 and the rear of No. 86.

Before leaving the works proper I will finish this section with a truly great photograph of those skilled inhabitants of the erecting shop posing beside a boiler of beautiful workmanship, all to be enjoyed in *Plate 68.* A great day for Melton.

I imagine many readers may never have seen or read a builder's authentic Specification for a steam locomotive engine. However by the courtesy of Messrs Hudswell, Clarke & Co. Ltd, I am able to reproduce one of their standard specifications which now follows. Although for a 0-6-0 tank engine, this specification would hold good for any other locomotive from the firm, including the 4-4-0 tank engines or the "Seven Sisters". In fact, having read such documents by other manufacturers it is quite obvious the British locomotive builders had agreed upon a tolerably common specification. The last heading is "Painting". This of course has to be loosely worded as details varied according to the customer's desires. In those days one must remember the buyer was always right!

Here I feel it most appropriate to illustrate in *Fig. 21* a typical Hudswell, Clarke builder's plate, the original now being in my collection. Although not off a Joint engine, No. 1869 was, like *Alpha* and *Vici* the "Capable Twins", a small saddle tank with outside cylinders 14in x 22in named *Betty* and went to the Oxfordshire Ironstone Company, Banbury on 30th June 1953.

Telegrams:- LOCO. LEEDS.
Telephone:- 20993. Two Lines.

CODES:- A.B.C. (4TH & 5TH EDITION.)
LIEBERS.-BENTLEYS-
A.I.- MARCONI-
ENGINEERING
STANDARDS.

Hudswell, Clarke & Co Ltd
RAILWAY FOUNDRY, LEEDS.

LOCOMOTIVE ENGINEERS.

Specification
OF A
Six Wheel Outside Cylinder Locomotive
Saddle TANK ENGINE

CYLINDERS *14* IN. DIA. *20* IN. STROKE. *6* WHEELS COUPLED *3* FT *4* INS. DIA.
GAUGE OF RAILWAY *4* FT *8½* INS.

General Description.   The Engine is of the outside cylinder class, the general arrangement being shewn by the accompanying *photo* "*Fords*" .... having *6* coupled wheels

Boiler.   The Boiler Barrel is *8* ft. *3* ins. long, and *3* ft. *6* ins. dia., the plates being *7/16* in. thick, secured by steel rivets on the vertical seams; the longitudinal seams having inside and outside butt strips, and double rivetted. The smoke-box tube plate to be *3/4* in. thick and flanged over to receive the smoke-box. All plates to be of the **best Siemens-Martin mild steel.** All holes drilled in position, all edges planed and hydraulic rivetted. The Boiler to be tested up to *240* lbs. per square in. by hydraulic pressure, and *180* lbs. per square in. steam pressure, being suitable for an ordinary working pressure of *160* lbs. per square in. A certificate of the boiler test being supplied. After being tested, and painted with anti-corrosive paint, the Boiler is lagged with yellow pine battens, on the top of which is fixed sheet-iron for protecting and neatly finishing the whole. The Barrel is firmly secured to the smoke-box by a strong steel angle ring.

Fire-box Casing.   The Fire-box Casing to be of the **best Siemens-Martin mild steel** plate, the covering sheet in one plate *7/16* in. thick, fire-door plate, *1/2* in. thick, and throat plate *9/16* in. thick, firmly rivetted together with steel rivets, the flanged plates being all **hydraulic flanged.** Foundation Ring to be a **hammered forging,** being machined in such places as are necessary for making joints. The Fire-hole Ring is **made weldless,** projecting so as to protect the edges of the copper plates. Mud plugs and mud doors are provided for cleaning purposes in suitable positions, and two safety plugs fitted. A steel seating is rivetted on the crown, which carries the safety valves and other mountings. **No mountings whatever are screwed directly into the Fire-box crown.**

Internal Fire-box.   The Internal Fire-box to be of the **best selected copper** *2* ft. *8½* ins. long, *3* ft. *0 7/8* ins. wide at top, and *3* ft. *4* ins. at bottom, and *4* ft. *6* ins. high at front, and *4* ft. *6* ins. at back, the crown and side being one plate. Thickness of plates: *7/16* in. thick, except that portion where the tubes pass through which is *3/4* in. thick. The plates are rivetted together with **best copper** rivets.

98

Staying. The Boiler is stayed with longitudinal stays running from the back of external fire-box to the smoke-box tube plate. The roof is supported by strong girder stays, properly slung from the shell, and accurately fitted to the box. Palm stays are also fixed, and the flat surfaces of the inner and outer fire-boxes by chased copper stays, $\frac{13}{16}$-in. dia., tightly screwed into both plates and rivetted over at each end, and pitched as near 4-ins. centre and centre as can be arranged.

Tubes. The Tubes to be _112_ in number, of the *b* **2** ins. dia. outside, No. _____ W.G. thick at the fire-box end, and gradually tapered down to No. _____ W.G. thick at the smoke-box end, being expanded at both ends, and ferruled with steel ferrules at the fire-box end. To be of the **best mixture** of metals, viz., 70% copper and 30% spelter.

Care is taken that the tubes are readily accessible for repairs and cleaning. They are placed in **vertical lines, thus accelerating steam generation, and preventing the accumulation of dirt between the tubes.**

Grate-bars. The Grate-bars are made of wrought-iron 1-in. wide at the top, $\frac{1}{2}$-in. at the bottom, and 4-ins. deep, with $\frac{1}{2}$-in. air spaces, and supported on a wrought-iron ring.

Fire-door. The Fire-door is of the compound sliding description, specially adapted for coal-burning.

Smoke-box. The Smoke-box is rivetted to the tube plate: sides and front $\frac{5}{16}$-in. thick, and door $\frac{3}{8}$-in. thick. The front plate is flanged for receiving the sides, the door being fitted with hinges, crossbar, lock-bolt, and handles. Steam-jet fitted, and controlled from driver's footplate.

Ashpan and Damper. Ashpan and Damper are fitted and provided with movable doors, worked by rods and levers from the driver's footplate, and attached to the underside of foundation ring of fire-box by means of angle-irons, studs, and cotters.

Regulator. The Regulator is fixed in the _Smokebox_ , and is so arranged as to be easily accessible, being controlled by a rod and handle from the footplate, the rod passing through back plate of Boiler with stuffing-box and brass gland.

Safety Valves. The Boiler is fitted with a pair of _"Pop"_ Safety Valves, arranged for a working pressure of _160_ lbs. per square inch, the seating being covered with a steel casing.

Mountings. The Engine is furnished with the following gun-metal fittings, viz., 2 Asbestos-packed Glass Water Gauge Cocks, fitted with polished Protectors; Whistle, Cylinder Tallow Cocks, Blow-off Cock, Steam Chest Cocks, Steam-pressure Gauge and Bracket, 2 Clack Boxes, _with stoppers._ All steam and water cocks being worked from the driver's footplate.

Feed Apparatus. The Boiler to be fed with 2 No. _7_ Injectors of our improved pattern, each of sufficient size to supply the Boiler.

Pipes. All Feed, Steam, and Delivery Pipes are of solid-drawn copper and fitted with brass flanges properly surfaced.

Chimney. The Chimney is of mild steel plate, and fitted with ornamental top.

Boiler Fixing. The Boiler is firmly fixed to the framing and cylinders at the smoke-box end, independently of any cylinder fixing bolts, expansion being provided for at the fire-box end by means of brackets and clasps. The Boiler being thus carried by the framing is very readily removed for purposes of repairs.

Framing. The frame plates to be of best mild steel $\frac{15}{16}$ ins. thick, **rolled in one piece,** extending the full length of the Engine; these are well braced together with suitable cross girders, having pieces slotted out in such places as will increase their elasticity without diminishing their strength. The whole, when completed, forming a strong elastic carriage, on which the Boiler rests without receiving the strains to which the framing is subjected.

Buffers. The Buffer-beams are of _Steel Plates 1¼" thick_, they are fitted with extra strong Buffers with wrought-iron heads and steel springs, and placed to suit existing stock, or if required Block Buffers can be attached.

Draw Gear. Draw-bars, Shackles, and Links, fitted at leading and trailing ends with springs and washers. Height, &c., arranged to suit existing stock.

Tank. The Tank to be of the _Saddle_ type, all rivets being countersunk, and securely fixed on the _top of Boiler_ , and to hold _680_ gallons of water.

Footplates. A platform of steel plates $\frac{1}{4}$-in. thick is fixed along each side and front of Engine, and supported by strong brackets rivetted to frames.

Bunker. A Coal Bunker is placed on the footplate _at back_ , having a capacity of _42_ cubic feet of fuel.

Driver's Shelter. Driver's Shelter to be of steel plates, fitted with spectacle glasses and brass frames.

Axle-boxes.

The Axle-boxes to be of strong cast-iron, of ample area on the sliding surface, and fitted with gun-metal bearings and syphon pipes complete, the bearings being properly fitted into the boxes, and provided with cast-iron keeps.

Horn Blocks.

The Horn Blocks to be of cast-iron, planed and accurately bedded to the frames, and held in position by bolts, turned so as to be a driving fit through both frames and horn blocks, all the holes being reamered out with the blocks in position.

Springs.

The Springs to be of the best spring steel, carefully adjusted over each wheel, and fastened with a buckle, and coupled to steel brackets on the frames by suitable wrought-iron links and pins. The Trailing Wheels are fitted with *a Cross Spring.*

Wheels and Axles.

The Wheels to be of tough cast-iron, accurately turned and bored _6_ in number, _3_ ft. _7_ ins. dia., fitted with tyres of the **best quality Siemens steel,** _2½_ ins. thick, and _5¼_ ins. wide, secured to the wheel-centres by means of screws after being properly shrunk on. The Axles to be **forgings of best Siemens-Martin steel,** with journals _6_ ins. dia. by _6½_ ins. long. The Wheels to be forced on the Axles by hydraulic pressure and afterwards properly keyed on. The Wheels are all turned to one diameter and gauge, the crank-pin holes being bored on a special machine. **The Axles and Tyres are made by well-known makers, the names being deeply branded.** *Driving Tyre flanges thinned to 5/8" thick.*

Crank-pins.

The Crank-pins to be **special Siemens steel,** got up with dead smooth surfaces, deeply case-hardened, ground-up true, and fixed into wheels by hydraulic pressure, both holes and crank-pins being taper.

Cylinders.

The Cylinders are outside the frames, of the **best cold blast cast-iron,** as hard as can be machined, accurately bored out to _14_ ins. dia. by _20_ ins. stroke, all joints being truly surfaced, so as to be steam-tight without the use of red lead. **The Cylinders, before being fitted into the frames, are coupled together, by means of a strong box casting containing the exhaust pipes, these being fixed to the frames by means of turned wrought-iron bolts fitted into reamered holes, keys being fitted in at each corner, when Cylinders are adjusted, for taking the strain off the bolts; this mode of fixing the Cylinders proving a sure method of preventing them from coming loose;** all glands and bushes are of the best gun-metal.

Pistons.

The Piston bodies are of cast-iron, fitted with 2 self-adjusting piston rings of the same material, the rods being of mild steel or wrought-iron, being securely fastened to Piston Body with a nut and safety pin.

Crosshead and Slide Bars.

The Crosshead to be of **the best Steel,** fitted with cast-iron slipper blocks with ample wearing surfaces. The Slide bars are of special steel secured to back cylinder cover with studs, brass liners being fitted between the bars and bracket, and to the motion plate brackets by recessed bolts into the bar and secured with nut and split pin.

Slide Valves.

The Slide Valves are of the same material as the cylinders, accurately planed and scraped to a true face, the valve spindles being made of the best mild steel or wrought-iron.

Valve Motion.

The Valve Motion is of the **"Stephenson"** link type, and worked by a weigh shaft above links, all the slot links, guides, suspension links, levers, and rod ends, being made of special steel, carefully fitted and then deeply **case-hardened,** after which they are refitted. Lubricators are provided solid with links. The motion is reversed by handle and quadrant fixed on driver's footplate, and these are also deeply case-hardened.

Eccentrics.

The Eccentrics are in halves and fitted with straps, of the best cast-iron, the lubricators being solid with the straps and finished with screwed covers

Connecting and Coupling Rods.

The Connecting and Coupling Rods are **solid forgings,** without weld from end to end, and made of mild steel, fitted with gun-metal bearings and cotters complete, and provided with oil cups for lubrication forged solid on, and finished with syphon pipes and screwed covers.

Brake.

The Engine is fitted with a powerful Hand-screw Brake controlled from the driver's footplate, and applied to _6_ wheels, the Brake Blocks are of cast-iron, so constructed as to wear on **that portion of the tyre which is not in constant contact with the rail,** thus wearing the tyres down more evenly and consequently lasting much longer; the hangers, shafts, crossbars, pins, etc., are of mild steel or wrought-iron, means being provided for taking up the wear of the blocks *Steam Brake fitted to work independently.*
Steam Brake R. H. Hand Brake L. H.

Sand-boxes.

Four Sand-boxes are fixed on the Engine, fitted with valves, rods, and levers, suitable for dry sand, the pipes extending down nearly to the rails, and the handles for actuating the same being controlled from the driver's footplate, the boxes being so arranged that the rails can be sanded in front of the wheels whilst the Engine is travelling either way.

Rail Guards.

Two strong wrought-iron Wheel Guards are securely bolted at each end of Engine.

Lubrication.

The Engine is fitted with 1 Automatic **Sight Feed Lubricator** for oiling the cylinders, regulator, and slide valves, which is controlled from the driver's footplate.

Lamps.	The Engine is provided with Head, Tail, Hand and Gauge Lamps, and suitable brackets for same are fixed.
Tools.	The following Tools are supplied with the Engine, viz.:—A Set of Firing Tools, and Small Crow-bar, Lock-up Tool Box, fixed on to footplate, containing a full Set of Screw Keys, 1 Lead and 1 Hand Hammer, 2 Chisels, 1 Pin Punch, 1 Drift, 1 Oil Bottle, 1 Large and 1 Small Oil Can, 1 Hand Brush, 1 Tallow Kettle
Painting.	The Engine to be well primed, rubbed down and neatly painted in colours, lined, and afterwards to receive 2 coats of varnish.

To M

HUDSWELL, CLARKE & CO. LTD.

Specification.

SUMMARY.

Dia. of Cylinders	*14*	ins.
Length of Stroke	*20*	ins.
Dia. of Wheels (C'pled)	*3* ft. *7*	ins.
	ft.	ins.
Wheel Base	*9* ft. *8*	ins.
Capacity of Tank	*680*	gallons.
Capacity of Coal-bunker	*42*	cub. ft.
Gauge of Railway	*4* ft. *8½*	ins.
Weight Empty	*23* tons. *11 cwts*	
Weight Loaded	*29* tons. *12* .	

Engine to take a curve of 95 ft radius.

HEATING SURFACE.

Firebox	*58·54*	sq. ft.
Tubes	*501·75*	sq. ft.
Total	*560·29*	sq. ft.
Grate Area	*8·5*	sq. ft.

15th June 1927

L 13437

Likewise in Fig. 22 is recorded a Sharp, Stewart builder's plate and similar to those fitted to all the Johnsonians for passengers. No. 4692 was constructed only four years after the Joint's No. 57, Sharp, Stewart No. 4196 and so only 496 engines later. I have no precise details of No. 4692 but the general opinion is that it was built for the Midland Railway.

Having been well acquainted with the M&GN all my life I feel a few reminiscences, mostly involving locomotives, may not be out of place. At one time I lodged with a retired Joint driver, the late Marshall Cartright of Lynn, when I was working in that ancient Borough. Usually I got the "Leicester" back from Norwich to South Lynn and I well remember our old friend, Peacock No. 24 leading four Midland bogies, touching a timed 72 mph down the Attlebridge Bank from Swannington Summit. This would equal the driving wheels turning over at about 337 rpm and even at this speed there was very little mechanical noise apparent and I was in the leading coach.

I can recollect one August morning c1922 at Hemsby station when a Peacock, I think No. 26, was to re-start the pick-up goods for Martham. Upon opening the regulator No. 26 crept forward one foot or so and then no more. The unflurried driver exchanged signs with the signalman and then reversed until the brake van was close to Ormesby distant signal. Then on a slight down grade, he made a good start and pounded through Hemsby on full regulator and what appeared to be full forward gear!

As many readers will know, the main line between Massingham and Hillington runs alongside the A148 main road. I recollect one morning when motor cycling back to Lynn I spied the "Leicester" accelerating through Massingham.

In those days road traffic was much less and I was able to keep neck and neck with No. 53 from Norwich shed until Hillington village street compelled me to give best to the express. Just to make sure I gave the rather hot OHV 680 an extra handpump full of oil. Later, George Brough was very interested, but pointed out that such bicycles were intended for such performances!

Whilst on the subject of train movements it was not uncommon on the Joint during the summer season at excursion times, for two long trains to be scheduled to pass at some wayside station. In several instances each train, probably of fourteen or more bogies, was too long for the passing loop. How did they pass? Let 'E' be the eastbound train to Yarmouth and 'W' the westbound train for South Lynn, as set out in *Fig. 23*. The procedure is as follows:

1) Train 'E' uncouples sufficient vehicles, left at 'L' to allow the engine and remainder to fill the loop 'M'. 2) Train 'W' moves forward on the main line past points 'P' and pushes coaches at 'L' as far as necessary, sometimes 20 chains or more, so that all is clear of points 'P'. 3) Train 'E' now shunts forward out of loop 'M' to a far distant point 'R', again sometimes 20/30 chains along the main line. 4) Train 'W' now reverses through the loop 'M', stops and leaves 'E's coaches in the loop. 5) Train 'W' then moves out of loop 'M' eastwards until locomotive and train are clear of point 'Q'. 6) Points now reset for main line and 'W' then proceeds towards South Lynn. 7) Train 'E' at 'R'

Top: Plate 68 A grand group in the Melton Works erecting shop, 1902.

Above left: Fig. 21 A Hudswell, Clarke & Co. Ltd builder's plate.

Above right: Fig. 22 A Sharp, Stewart & Co. Ltd builder's plate.

now reverses into loop 'M', couples up the left remaining bogies, reverses and starts off out of loop and accelerates towards Yarmouth. In some cases as many as eight bogies would have to be left in the loop 'M' which meant that during movement (4) the locomotive would have to shift a probable total of more than 22 coaches! A goodly achievement for a four-coupled engine and testimony to Melton's maintenance.

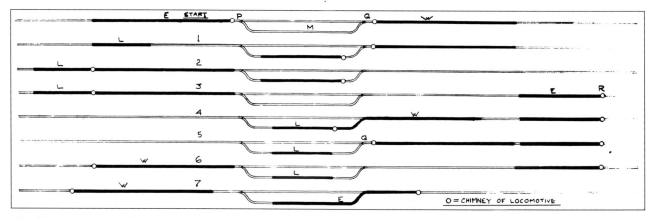

Fig. 23 **Train crossing diagram.**

During the floods of 1912 my late father, H.O. Clark, had to travel from Norwich to Yarmouth and as the GER was closed he journeyed via Melton. However at Stalham the stationmaster informed the driver there was about a foot of water between Catfield and Martham and it was up to him to chance it. The driver, name now unknown, did chance it, took the flooded length dead slow and eventually arrived safely at Yarmouth Beach. My father's chief memory was of an agitated farmer at Hemsby awaiting a prize-winning gilt travelling with plenty of straw in the guard's van! In those days all railways carried anything without demur.

Besides football excursions and errands of mercy, a Peacock, in this instance No. 25, gained a measure expressive of pleasure by hauling a special excursion to Yarmouth from Melton Constable. The great occasion was Queen Victoria's Jubilee and in *Plate 69* we see No. 25 spotless and suitably decorated, ready to convey a happy populace to a day of innocent enjoyment beside the seaside.

Although hardly a locomotive, a Sentinel railcar was working on the Joint during the summer of 1933 being first introduced during July that year and numbered LNER 248. It was built in 1932 and had vacuum operated mounting steps and for some time was known as *Tantivy*. Such machines usually had a six cylinder engine with poppet valves and at busy times drew a trailer, thus reducing its normal top speed of up to 70mph, naturally to much less. The boiler was of the Yarrow water tube type and injector-fed. Its usual area of activity was the Yarmouth-Stalham section. For about a year or more another similar car worked a local Norwich-Drayton service, so conveniently timed that certain Norwich businessmen were known to return home to Dray-

Fig. 24 **Proposed 2-6-2T locomotive for the M&GN.**

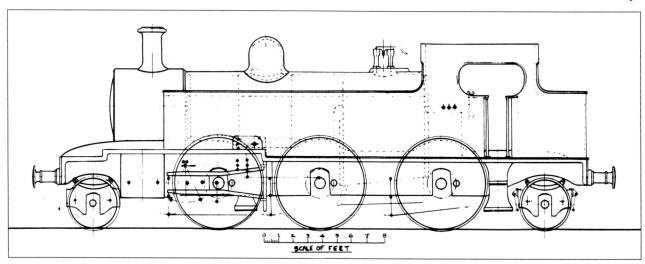

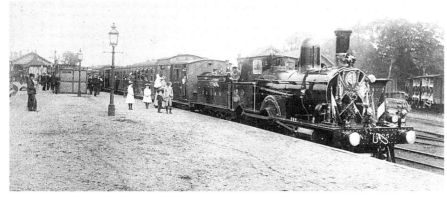

Plate 69 Beyer, Peacock 4-4-0 No. 25 on the Queen Victoria Jubilee train.

ton for lunch, as the Sentinel was rostered to stand just over an hour at Drayton. Usually 48 passengers could be accommodated in each car. Apparently the next year saw a LNWR slip coach in use also. I have refrained from using space on further details, as unlike some more deserving Joint engines, these railcars are adequately covered in the popular technical press to which I would refer the reader. According to the builders, valve tappet clearance was most important and a feeler gauge was provided in the back inside cover of the driver's instruction manual. I am happy to say my copy has such a gauge.

Returning now to locomotives proper, I find it most interesting to record that a new, special Derby design for a suitable "maid of all work" for the Joint was designed and drawn out by Mr W. Moore of the Derby Works drawing office and this drawing was completed on 30th September 1914. I have prepared an outline drawing suitable for reproduction seen in *Fig. 24* and this engine would have had the following main dimensions:

Cylinders	19in x 24in
Driving wheels, dia.	6ft
Leading and trailing wheels, dia.	3ft 3$\frac{1}{2}$in
Wheelbase, leading to first driving	8ft 6in
Wheelbase, driving	6ft 11in + 8ft 2in
Wheelbase, driving total coupled	15ft 1in
Wheelbase, rear driving to trailing	7ft
Wheelbase, total	30ft 7in
CL of buffers above rail level	3ft 5in
Length of buffers	1ft 9$\frac{3}{4}$in
Length overall, over buffers	39ft 4$\frac{1}{2}$in
Height of running plate above rail	4ft 8in
Height of running plate above cylinders	5ft 2in
Boiler MR type B. Superheated.	
Boiler Working pressure	160psi
Heating surface, firebox	110sq ft
Heating surface, tubes	735sq ft
Heating surface, total	845sq ft
Heating surface, superheater	290sq ft
Superheated steam temperature	500°F
Grate area	17.5sq ft
Smokebox O/D	4ft 11$\frac{1}{8}$in
Height to top of chimney above rail level	13ft 2$\frac{9}{16}$ in
Height to CL boiler above rail level	8ft
Side and bunker tanks capacity	1,750gall
Coal bunker capacity	2ton
Weights in W.O. leading wheels	8ton 10cwt
Weights in W.O. leading driving	16ton 18cwt
Weights in W.O. centre driving	17ton 5cwt
Weights in W.O. trailing driving	16ton 18cwt
Weights in W.O. trailing wheels	8ton 9cwt
Weights in W.O. total	68ton
Weights in W.O. coupled wheels	51ton 1cwt
Tractive effort @ 80%	15,402lb = 6.87ton

Clever as this design was, one must remember the type B Boiler was not converted to a Belpaire form until two years later, in the guise of a G6 and using dry saturated steam. Then the superheated version was not available for 15 years after that, to constitute type G6S. Had this new design been made all these years later the boiler would probably have been pressed to 200psi. Some critics complained of the driving wheels being 6ft diameter whereas they might have been say, 5ft 3in. Certainly the tractive effort would have been increased but I feel that the estimated 15,402lb would have suited the Joint very well. The intention may have been to use say six such locomotives to form the class for fast local traffic being moved to Melton Constable from the other three termini. There it would be amalgamated into a "Leicester" say of twelve bogie stock and taken forward by new replicas of the Johnsons with their famous G7 or similar boiler. But it would have been absorbingly interesting to have observed them at work. I could have enjoyed riding on one and taking a few indicator diagrams when working up Rudham Bank which would have ensured a perfect day!

Although I have included brief general mention of the histories of those firms which produced locomotive engines for the Joint, I feel a few further details of the individual chiefs concerned may not be out of place. Henry Dübs for instance was born in Guntersblum, Germany, in 1816. Coming to England in 1839 he spent a period in the drawing office at Sharp Roberts Ltd, eventually becoming a partner with Walter Montgomerie Neilson as mentioned previously.

Samuel Waite Johnson was born in Leeds in 1831, served some time with E.B. Wilson in the same city and later worked under Archibald Sturrock on the GNR at Peterborough. He moved to Stratford in 1866 to take charge of the GER locomotive department. He was there designing his successful 2-4-0 tender and 0-4-4 tank engines until he made his final move to Derby, to succeed Matthew Kirtley, in 1873. Then followed his series of MR locomotives celebrated for their mechanical and aesthetic excellence. So excellent were they that it gave rise to that typical comment "Typical Johnson".

A very interesting item of history fits in appropriately at this point and tying up with Neilson and Johnson. When No. 59 was completed it was shunted outside the General Offices of Hyde Park Works and served as a background to a very important visitor viz His Excellency Li Hung Chang, Minister of the Interior for China and the happy party is shown in *Plate 70*. The date of the visit was Tuesday 18th August 1896. His Excellency is seated centrally in the front row flanked on each side by his aides and interpreter. Standing on the footplate is Mr Hugh Reid who became senior partner in 1894, later becoming Sir Hugh Reid, Baronet. All the visitors who arrived by special train, were taken completely through all the shops and departments of the works, and Li Hung Chang expressed himself hugely pleased with all that he had seen and for his sincere reception. Upon leaving in their special train they "departed amidst the cheers of the workmen and others". I have not discovered what orders resulted from this almost "State" visit and occasion, but one may assume the order book benefited therefrom.

A very pertinent point I must make is that in this year, 1896, the United Kingdom was leading the world in locomotive manufacture and design. At the time of writing, 1987, China is the only country with sufficient courage and enterprise to be still building large steam locomotive engines. How a piston has travelled full stroke!

In early 1987 a member of the M.&G.N. Circle, having journeyed via the Trans-Siberian Railway to China, was able to present a copy of *Plate 70* to the only Railway Museum in that country. I understand it was received with interest and gratitude.

Deeley chimneys were common at Melton, being one small item by which some Johnson engines were modified by Richard Mountford Deeley. Mr Deeley succeeded S.W. Johnson in 1904, finally retiring in 1909. Besides locomotives proper he developed a water softening plant in collaboration with the company's chief chemist Mr Leonard Archbutt. Richard Deeley lived to the great age of 89 years and died in 1944.

Recollecting the Ivatt contribution in Chapter XII it is interesting to note that Henry Alfred Ivatt was born a Cambridgeshire man in 1851, an area close to that covered by the Joint, and at the age of seventeen was apprenticed at

Crewe under John Ramsbottom. Subsequently he was Works Manager and Locomotive Superintendent to the GS&WR of Ireland under John Aspinall, later taking over as chief at Inchicore when Mr Aspinall left to become CME of the Lancashire & Yorkshire Railway. In 1895 Henry Ivatt was offered the post of Chief Locomotive Engineer to the GNR and he took up this important position in March 1896. Additional to producing the first British Atlantic type engine, he redesigned several types of 0-6-0 goods locomotives, not the least important being the design we have enjoyed studying in *Fig. 18.* Mr Ivatt died at his home in Haywards Heath in 1922.

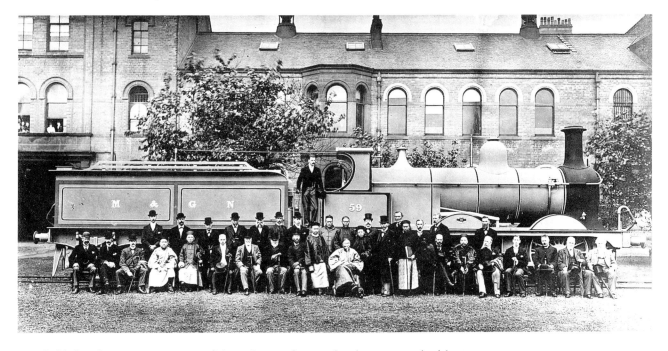

I think a few notes on some of the other engineers closely connected with the Joint will help to complete this section. Wilkinson & Jarvis it will be remembered were the contractors who made the original Great Yarmouth & Stalham Light Railway in 1875 onwards, and which was worked by the "Bristol Rovers". James John Wilkinson was the son of Dr Garth Wilkinson, a Swede settled in England. James Thomas Jarvis, born a Devonian, became a pupil on the South Devon Railway. After the creation of their partnership they had offices, most appropriately, at 3 Victoria Street, Westminster. They surveyed the route of the line originally and were later the contractors for the Lynn & Fakenham line. For making the North Walsham extension they made temporary site offices in Briggate Gate House at Honing. It was here and at this time that a young William Marriott joined them.

Plate 70 **The Chinese group pose alongside Johnson 0-6-0 No. 59 at Neilson's Hyde Park Works, Glasgow on 18th August 1896.**

Mr William E. Newman joined the old E&MR in 1881 after answering an advertisement for a draughtsman. He soon became personal assistant to Mr Marriott on the formation of the Joint in 1893. I had the pleasure of meeting Mr Newman on a number of occasions and learnt that he was sent to Pine House Commercial School in Wincanton where his father, also William, took him on to be apprenticed, Mr Newman senior being a mechanical engineer and contractor. His father gave him a good grounding which enabled him to gain further experience with the Somerset & Dorset Joint Railway from 1885 to 1890. It was there he answered the advertisement already referred to and which led him to Melton. He was the first draughtsman there and instituted the first steam heating for passenger coaches on Norfolk lines. He also introduced the Whitaker exchange tablet apparatus and the first dining car service to Sheringham. Perhaps one of his most important jobs was the design and draughting work to convert the Sharp, Stewart Cornish engines into the class of the "Nine Brothers". When Mr Marriott retired in 1924 Mr Newman was his obvious successor. For many years he resided in Sheringham with his devoted sister keeping house for him. He was proud of the fact that he could trace his ancestry back to the original Le-Niweman in 1327.

When Mr Newman retired in 1932 he was succeeded by Mr Albert Henry

Nash who had been apprenticed at Swindon Works, becoming an analytical chemist in the laboratory and then a draughtsman in the main drawing office. After a spell with the Gloucester Carriage & Wagon Company he returned to Swindon as leading draughtsman and assistant Locomotive Works Manager. He next enjoyed a spell with the Federated Malay States Railways and with the Batu Caves Portland Cement Works, British Malaya. In World War I he served on HMS *Caledon* and HMS *King George V.* After the war he became manager of J.J. Saville's Triumph Steel Works in Sheffield, later moving on to the old LYR Carriage & Wagon Department at Newton Heath, where he was Chief Wagon Foreman from 1924 to 1928. In the latter year he was appointed Leading Draughtsman and when the plant closed down he was fortunate, as he told me, to be appointed Resident Mechanical Engineer at Melton Constable, in 1932 and to succeed Mr Newman. After the run-down on Melton Works in 1936 Mr Nash left the next year to become First Assistant to the Works Superintendent at Derby Locomotive Works and in 1942 became Assistant Works Superintendent whence he retired on 30th June 1945.

I well remember helping Mr Nash to find a house to rent in Norwich just after he took charge at Melton. After a temporary period he moved to other accommodation.

Mr Nash was a great supporter of the Royal British Legion and another interest was the life of Col. T.E. Lawrence (of Arabia). On one occasion I helped him improve the brake on the locomotive coal joist at Melton. In concluding my references to this gentleman I must admit I never really liked his design of locomotive chimney! A member of the Institution of Locomotive Engineers, Mr Nash lived until 1947.

Lastly we have to remember and praise the Chief of Melton I have referred to so often – Mr William Marriott. According to one of his daughters Mrs Ryder Smith, recently deceased, her father was born in Basle in 1857 where his father was professor of English at that university. On account of his parents' death he came to Bideford in Devon where he went to school, when aged only eleven. To some extent he took after his father for languages and was quite fluent in French, Latin, German and Greek. He knew also a little Italian. In Bideford he lived, adopted by an aunt. He had attended a Moravian school at Neuwied and Lausanne for a short time because of his mother's Swiss-German origin. After finally leaving school in England he started as an engineering pupil with Ransomes & Rapier Ltd, Waterside Works, Ipswich from 1875-79. This famous firm had made several small locomotives for the Shanghai & Woosung Railway in China and later became renowned for their large steam travelling locomotive breakdown cranes. After leaving Ransomes & Rapier and with this training behind him he became a pupil of Mr R.H. Hill, MICE a civil engineer in London, but he returned to Ransomes & Rapier as a mechanical engineering draughtsman. He left Ipswich upon being appointed engineer and contractor's agent with and for Messrs Wilkinson & Jarvis at 3 Victoria Street, Westminster as we have noticed. It was thus that he came to Norfolk in 1881 in connection with the surveying and making of the GY&SLR. Thus began his life-long association with East Anglia. Almost as soon as the E&MR was formed in 1883 he was appointed engineer and a year later Locomotive Superintendent. He was also very good at Parliamentary work and negotiated among several projects the Lynn Loop in 1885 and the construction of the Cromer line in 1887. In addition to all this he found time to carry out an amount of private consulting work. The then general manager of the E&MR was Mr J.J. Petrie and upon his death, Mr Marriott was given the job of Engineer & Traffic Manager as from 1st January 1919. Mr Marriott eventually retired on 31st December 1924 and died in his home at Roquebrune, 8 Cromer Road, Sheringham on 18th November 1943. After his retirement and, as so often happens, (it was so in my own father's case), his position was split up when Mr W. Newman became resident mechanical engineer and Mr A.E. Langley resident civil engineer.

Mr Marriott married in 1885, shortly after coming to Norfolk and his family comprised four sons, Robert, Aubrey, Frank and Stanley, complemented by three daughters. Robert was apprenticed in Melton shops and later became responsible for most of the work for the M1 motorway. Aubrey and Frank both qualified in the medical profession but Stanley was a World War I casualty.

Plate 71 **Mr and Mrs William Marriott.**

TO THE MEMORY OF

WILLIAM MARRIOTT M.I.C.E. M.I.M.E. M.R.SAN. I.

ENGINEER & LOCOMOTIVE SUPT. E & M RLY 1883-1893
M & GN JT RLY 1893-1919

ENGINEER & MANAGER   M & GN JT RLY 1919-1924
BORN 1857 DIED 1943

ERECTED BY THE M & GN CIRCLE 1973

Plate 72 **The memorial plaque to Mr William Marriott at 8 Cromer Road, Sheringham.**

In the early days, as noticed already, locomotives were painted various shades of green with the smaller engines black. It was Mrs Marriott who suggested that, as so much of the Norfolk countryside was brilliant with golden gorse *(Ulex europaeus)* much of the year, it would be a distinctive livery for the larger locomotive engines and this suggestion was adopted. How very fine

Plate 73 North Walsham station in its halcyon days as Johnson 4-4-0 No. 12 enters with an anglers' train in the 1890s.

Plate 74 Beyer, Peacock 4-4-0, Class A No. 26 coming off Cross Keys Bridge in the late 1930s.

all the express engines looked as they performed their tasks of haulage. But I must point out that by golden gorse is meant, not the colour of a single flower but the deep impressive golden tint when seen by the acre or in the mass. Here I think the picture in *Plate 71* expressed better than many words the great man and his lifelong consort.

For some years the M.&G.N. Circle were acutely aware that no memorial to Melton's chief had been established and so the Circle, at their own cost,

had made and placed on the wall of 8 Cromer Road, Sheringham, the bronze plaque illustrated in *Plate 72*. This was unveiled on 8th December 1973 by – so appropriately – the Chief's illustrious son, now Sir Robert Marriott. All present regretted there was no *Parvo cristatus* present in the sidings opposite to give three true peals on its whistle!

Neither has Mr Marriott been forgotten by officialdom. In the autumn of 1984 part of the old trackbed of the Norwich-Melton Constable line from Marlpit Lane to the River Wensum bridge, beyond Attlebridge station, was opened as a public footpath and christened Marriott's Way, a pleasant and picturesque walk of 7 miles and 3 chains. Additionally, a new village to be called Thorpe Marriott was commenced to be built at the same time in an area between the Fakenham and Reepham Roads in Taverham, to accommodate 2,000 dwellings. The title was suggested by Mr Edwin Spalding of Taverham, the area involved being 99 acres. It is very gratifying that an engineer – for a change – is so permanently memorialised.

As a fitting tribute to the Joint as a railway I think the delightful country station scene at North Walsham, depicted in *Plate 73* records how important the line was in earlier days and the service given to the populace at large.

Just as important if not more so in many ways was the great tonnage of goods moved about all over the system, and I feel a fitting conclusion will be made by one of my own favourite pictures in *Plate 74,* of Peacock No. 26 coming off Cross Keys Bridge with a typical goods train bound for the East.

Appendix A

Locomotive Stock List of the Eastern & Midlands Railway

December 1883

E&MR No.	Type	Builder	Builder's No.	Date Built	Previous Owners	Previous Name Number
1	0-6-0T	Sharp, Stewart	2372	1874	1) CMR 2) L&FR	17 1 Melton Constable
2	0-6-0T	Sharp, Stewart	2371	1874	1) CMR 2) L&FR	16 2 Reepham
3	0-6-0T	Sharp, Stewart	2370	1874	1) CMR 2) L&FR	15 3 Blakeney
4	0-4-0ST	Hudswell, Clarke & Rodgers	183	1878	Wilkinson & Jarvis	Alpha
5	0-4-0ST	Hudswell, Clarke & Rodgers	192	1880	Wilkinson & Jarvis	Vici
6	0-6-0ST	Black, Hawthorn	503	1881	L&FR	Holt
7	0-6-0ST	Black, Hawthorn	416	1877	1) Y&NNR 2) L&FR	Ida
8	4-4-0T	Hudswell, Clarke & Rodgers	209	1878	L&FR	Hillington
9	4-4-0T	Hudswell, Clarke & Rodgers	211	1879	L&FR	Fakenham
10	4-4-0T	Hudswell, Clarke & Rodgers	224	1880	L&FR	Norwich
11	0-6-0T +Tender	Sharp, Stewart	2360	1874	1) CMR 2) L&FR	
12	0-6-0T +Tender	Sharp, Stewart	2361	1874	1) CMR 2) L&FR	
13	0-6-0T +Tender	Sharp, Stewart	2368	1874	1) CMR 2) L&FR	
14	0-6-0T +Tender	Sharp, Stewart	2369	1874	1) CMR 2) L&FR	
15	0-6-0ST	Fox, Walker	333	1877	Y&NNR	Ormesby
16	0-6-0ST	Fox, Walker	338	1877	Y&NNR	Stalham
17	0-6-0ST	Black, Hawthorn	517	1881	Y&NNR	Aylsham
18	0-6-0T +Tender	Sharp, Stewart	2373	1874	1) CMR 2) L&FR	

19	4-4-0T	Hudswell, Clarke & Rodgers	232	1881	Y&NNR	Great Yarmouth
20	4-4-0T	Hudswell, Clarke & Rodgers	231	1881	L&FR	King's Lynn
21	4-4-0	Beyer, Peacock	2105	1882	L&FR	
22	4-4-0	Beyer, Peacock	2106	1882	L&FR	
23	4-4-0	Beyer, Peacock	2107	1882	L&FR	
24	4-4-0	Beyer, Peacock	2108	1882	L&FR	
25	4-4-0	Beyer, Peacock	2338	1883	-	
26	4-4-0	Beyer, Peacock	2339	1883	-	
27	4-4-0	Beyer, Peacock	2340	1883	-	
28	4-4-0	Beyer, Peacock	2341	1883	-	
29	2-4-0	Rothwell, Hick & Rothwell	160	1857	L&CR LNWR	3 Sedgewick 1118/1101
30	2-4-0	Rothwell, Hick & Rothwell	165	1857	L&CR LNWR	8 Luck of Edenhall 1802/1112
31	4-4-0T	Hudswell, Clarke & Rodgers	210	1879	Y&NNR	Martham
32	4-4-0T	Hudswell, Clarke & Rodgers	208	1878	Y&NNR	North Walsham

Abbreviations:

CMR	Cornwall Minerals Railway
L&CR	Lancaster & Carlisle Railway
L&FR	Lynn & Fakenham Railway
LNWR	London & North Western Railway
Y&NNR	Yarmouth & North Norfolk Railway

Appendix B

Locomotive Stock on the M&GN at the Time of Mr W. Marriott's Retirement

31st December 1924

Class	Type	Cylinder Position	Builder (Designer)	Date Built	Running Numbers
A	4-4-0	outside	Beyer, Peacock	1882	21-24
				1883	25-28
				1886	29-31
				1888	32-35
B	4-4-0T	outside	Hudswell, Clarke & Rodgers	1879	9A
				1881	20A
C	4-4-0	inside	Sharp, Stewart (S. W. Johnson)	1894	1-7, 11-14, 17-18, 36-39
				1896	42-57
C	4-4-0	inside	Beyer, Peacock (S. W. Johnson)	1899	74-80
D	0-6-0	inside	Neilson & Co. (S. W. Johnson)	1896	58-65
D	0-6-0	inside	Kitson & Co. (S. W. Johnson)	1899	66-73
DA	0-6-0	inside	Dübs & Co. (H. A. Ivatt)	1900	81-92
-	0-6-0T	outside	M&GNJR Melton Constable (W. Marriott)	1897	14A
				1898	1A
				1899	3A, 11A
				1900	15
				1902	12A, 17A
				1903	2A
				1905	16
-	4-4-2T	outside	M&GNJR Melton Constable (W. Marriott)	1904	41
				1909	9, 20
-	0-6-0ST	outside	Fox, Walker	1877	16A

8, 10, 19 and 40 not used at this time

Bibliography

Beyer, Peacock Quarterly Reviews
British Locomotive Builders, J.W. Lowe
Eastern Daily Press
Engineer, The
Engineering
English Mechanics
Forty Years on a Norfolk Railway, W. Marriott
Great Eastern Railway Magazine
History of the Great Northern Railway, C.H. Grinling
Institution of Civil Engineers, Proceedings
Institution of Locomotive Engineers, Proceedings
Institution of Mechanical Engineers, Proceedings
Kitsons of Leeds, E. Kitson Clark
Locomotive & Train Working in the Latter Part of the Nineteenth Century, E.L. Ahrons
Locomotive Magazine, The
Lynn News & Advertiser
Midland & Great Northern Joint Circle, Bulletins, drawings and photographs
Midland Railway, C. Stretton
Midland Railway Locomotive Album, 1880-1910 J.H. Wright
Modern Railways
National Railway Museum Records – York
Newcomen Society, The Transactions
Norfolk Chronicle, The
Norfolk Railway Society Newsletters
Railways
Railway Engineer, The
Railway Engineers, J. Marshall
Railway Gazette, The
Railway Magazine, The
Railway Museum Records – Clapham
Railway Museum Records – Section 284/3
Stephenson Locomotive Society, Journals

Abbreviations

Railway companies

CMR	Cornwall Minerals Railway
CV&HR	Colne Valley & Halstead Railway
E&MR	Eastern & Midlands Railway
GER	Great Eastern Railway
GNR	Great Northern Railway
GS&WR	Great Southern & Western Railway (Ireland)
GY&SLR	Great Yarmouth & Stalham Light Railway
L&CR	Lancaster & Carlisle Railway
L&FR	Lynn & Fakenham Railway
LNWR	London & North Western Railway
LTSR	London, Tilbury & Southend Railway
LYR	Lancashire & Yorkshire Railway
MR	Midland Railway
M&GN	Midland & Great Northern Joint Railway
NER	North Eastern Railway
Y&NNR	Yarmouth & North Norfolk Railway

Tables of dimensions

CL	Centre line
dia	diameter
L.H.	Left Hand
L.H.S	Left Hand Side
O/D	Outside Diameter
PSI	Pounds per square inch
R.H.	Right Hand
W.O.	Working Order
W.P.	Working Pressure

Index